THE MAN WHO FELL
INTO A PUDDLE

THE MAN WHO FELL INTO A PUDDLE

ISRAELI LIVES

Igal Sarna

Translated from the Hebrew by Haim Watzman

Pantheon Books, New York

To Smadar, Noam, and Anat

Library of Congress Cataloging-in-Publication Data

Sarna, Igal, 1952–
[Makom shel Osher. English]
The man who fell into a puddle: Israeli lives /
Igal Sarna; translated from the Hebrew by Haim
Watzman.
p. cm .
ISBN 0-375-42062-2
I. Watzman, Haim.   II. Title.
PJ5055.4.A77 M3513 2002   892.4′36—DC21   2002022428

www.pantheonbooks.com

Book designed by Johanna Roebas

Printed in the United States of America

First American Edition
2   4   6   8   9   7   5   3   1

CONTENTS

Contents

PREFACE

THERE HAD NEVER BEEN as many policemen at the
gates to Tel Aviv's military cemetery as there were this
year. It was Memorial Day and I was there with a
fellow soldier from the Yom Kippur War—two middle-
aged men visiting the grave of a twenty-year-old comrade with whom they had fought in a tank brigade
nearly three decades ago. A policeman at the entrance
asked me if I was carrying a weapon. "No," I replied, "I'm
not armed."

Mourning itself had become dangerous. There
were warnings about possible terrorist attacks on funer-
als. The past had blurred. In the spring of 2002, I was
no longer sure if the '73 war, in which my friend Mintz
was killed, had been the beginning of a peace process,
as we had thought until recently, or whether the wars

were just piling up, one on top of the other, like abandoned suitcases in a lost and found department.

A fear that we had never known before, or, perhaps, the same specter of fear I have followed for years in my stories of survivors, has permeated our lives in the last year and a half. The conflict has triumphed over the peace settlement. Anger surfaced and with it, its sister, revenge, the poison passion that muddles clear thought. For a year and a half, I've been a war journalist, moving between the sides, going from Tel Aviv to Bethlehem and Ramallah. I no longer feel at ease writing stories of families or accounts of the past. Torn away from my regular writing, sometimes frightened, I go into the heart of darkness. Traveling to the place where two enraged tribes, one of them my own, clutch at each other's throats. Only there, in the unrest, in the noise of shooting, do I find my place as a documentary writer who must to tell what he sees. I write, I speak incessantly with people about the situation. Even good friends have a hard time agreeing now about how it all started.

Life seems to go on. I get up in the morning and take my eight-year-old daughter to school. We go hand in hand. Walking quickly. She is deep in her sweet affairs, I in my bitter ones. We pass through a broad boulevard and a narrow street, until we reach the new armed guard at the entrance to her school. He asks me to open the case of my laptop, to check. My daughter says to me: "We're lucky no one from our family was killed." She is preoccupied with the terrorist attacks. She builds a protected life for herself in her room, doesn't go to crowded places, but is very preoccupied with death. In the middle of the night, she comes to our bed, weeping from a nightmare. She nods off, but I find it hard to fall asleep again.

I leave her at school and go to my café, before work. I sit alone in a place that used to be buzzing with people. Many are afraid. Places of entertainment have become targets for terrorists. The owner of my café, Charlie, has decided not to hire a guard. Most of the cafés and restaurants have a man, armed with a revolver and a metal detector, standing at the door. Sometimes I joke with Charlie, suggesting that he take down the heavy sacks of coffee from South America he stores on the second floor, and put them below, as a protective wall. He now stands at the door himself, as a guard, using his own body to ward off any danger to the café he built with all of his savings, when he came back here after living for years in Boston.

Charlie guards the door and I scrutinize everyone who enters. Once these were glances of desire, or curiosity, but now it's fear. There's no longer a clear profile of a suicide bomber: a boy, a girl, a man. Anything is possible. My mother phones me from her old-age home: "What's going to happen?" she asks me, this eighty-six-year-old woman who immigrated to this country seventy-two years ago to build a safe home. She doesn't wait for an answer. "It's a good thing your father didn't live to see this," she consoles herself.

The two barmen, who have no work to do, stand next to the espresso machine, arguing about what to do about Yasser Arafat—deport him or exterminate him. I look through the café window at the old building across the road. New graffiti, sixty years of layers of paint, an old man on the balcony. A poster about a new exhibition. I feel a sudden sense of calm. Sometimes in the narrative of a nation, as in the life story of a person, there are those bad years, in which everything seems to be going haywire. Afterwards, somehow, things get back on track. The disaster becomes a memory; the memory, a story. Throughout my life as a journalist, I have written about Israeli traumas and have seen how new lives are built on the ruins. How a new land sprouts out from a charred ground zero. In the military cemetery too, at the grave of my friend Mintz, who was killed by a tank shell, I spoke with his younger brother about my dead comrade's childlike ways, and how, if he were to return today, he wouldn't recognize the place where he was born. The brother's two daughters, standing between the mourners and the soldiers, laughed with us at the pranks of the uncle they had never met.

THE MAN WHO FELL
INTO A PUDDLE

ZE'EV

TOWARD THE BEGINNING OF DECEMBER, when people rush down New York streets puffing mist, and skyscraper tops vanish into a spongy sky, the police on Staten Island picked up the body of a forty-year-old man. He was tall, slightly balding, and had a mustache. The facial features were sharp and striking. Documents found on him indicated he was an Israeli citizen.

Relatives were located in Tel Aviv and the body was flown to Israel. A cousin came to the morgue and identified the dead man, whose good looks had barely altered over the years. He rested, clean and shaved, in his coffin, as if he had hopped over for a quick visit home.

Two days later a dozen or so men and women walked behind the coffin in the Yarkon cemetery and interred the boy who had come back from America after a long absence—just a few graves away from his sister, who had hanged herself only two months previously. Both of them in the same row. There was only the family there—those who had survived the Holocaust, who had together endured the Lodz Ghetto and the lagers and come to Israel. Here they had large families that got together to celebrate Pesach around a table groaning with good things. The rabbi, as expected, said a few words, commended the soul of Ze'ev, the son of Avraham, to heaven, and warned the demons and liliths against disturbing his repose.

No death announcements appeared in the newspapers, nor were notices tacked onto trees, so none of the dead man's friends knew of his demise. People continued to wonder where Ze'ev Izbitzky—the guy people had once nicknamed "God"—had disappeared to. What was he doing in New York, which had swallowed him up in the seventies after his return from Tibet? I'm talking about people who had been looking for him for years—like his school buddies Schwartz and Bar Natan. All of them now had families and adolescent kids of about the age when they themselves had gotten to know Ze'ev and had sat whole nights with him on the road-guard railings at the corner arguing about Ayn Rand's books and their chances of conquering the world, or, alternatively, scoring a hamburger at Wimpy's and getting away without paying.

Two months after Ze'ev was buried—almost surreptitiously, it seemed—I heard about his death. I shot out of my chair, because an image of Ze'ev the boy popped up from my childhood memories. He was black-haired, with oblique eyes, and lived on a back street where there were two synagogues. Ze'ev was deemed the one who would realize all his dreams, the dreams he confabulated in his Polish parents' ground-floor apartment, which had a terrace that faced the Ashkenazi synagogue and the concrete bomb shelter. From that moment I could not rest. I began going around among friends and neighbors and among those who remained from the generation of Ze'ev's parents in the neighborhood and elsewhere, and in the labor federation's dues-collection bureau, where his father had worked. I approached people who had seen him or had known his sister Esther, his classmates, and the psychiatrist in New York who had tried to save him.

The details accumulated, amassed, and, in their still, small voices, told stories that sometimes contradicted one another. No Izbitzkys remained to tell about the family, or what had gone on in the house on Ben-Yehuda Street that led, ultimately, to such a bad end. I heard many whispers, some of them murky. All spoke of four—the father and mother, Avraham and Shula, who came from the Holocaust, and of the children, Esther and Ze'ev, who were given the names of dead people from over there. Now no one was left, no vestige of any of the four—no children or grandchildren who might have remained to tell. There was his sister's apartment in north Tel Aviv that stood empty, an inheritance worth easily half a million dollars that waited for Ze'ev while he wandered homeless through New York. The

Izbitzkys were exterminated, after the war, by a bomb on a fifty-year timer.

"They were good and honest people. But Auschwitz is very hard," the neighbor Clara told me. She'd lived above them all those years, also in a rent-controlled home. At the time we were born, in 1952, half the homes in Tel Aviv were acquired through the convenient method of "key money," in which you buy, for a modest sum, the right to enjoy low-rent housing. Almost everyone I knew as a boy lived on the ground floor.

"It's a kind of fear that came from there," Clara said, "that created all kinds of complications in their heads." She shook her own head from side to side to show how confused they were from the Holocaust. "Sick from the camps. Good people, but not normal. I couldn't shake out a rug without Izbitzky screaming, and you needed a lot of tact when dealing with them." The neighbors described Shula, the mother, as a short woman, soft and fretful, ineffectual when confronted by her husband. For her life was hard, something to be gotten through somehow. She'd endured all the horrors of the Lodz Ghetto, and then the camps, along with her sisters. They saved each other and came here after the war, five sisters who stuck close together.

In Israel, Shula met Avraham Izbitzky, a man a head taller than she, gaunt like a hermit, and strict, who had come from "there" without anyone. He bore dark memories. What had he been through there? What had happened to him? Whom had he lived with and what had he done? A bit of this came out in testimony he gave in a

Holocaust trial in Tel Aviv in 1963. There were those who said that he had been a hero "there" and had helped Jews; and there were those who whispered the opposite. Some survivors reeked of the camps all their lives; the horror stuck to their flesh like a second skin.

Three years after the Holocaust, the daughter, Esther, was born in Tel Aviv, and Avraham began working in the labor federation's dues bureau, where he rose to the position of director of the collections department. He was an official who loved order. His friends from work would remember him well as something of a vocal impressionist who told jokes and only on rare occasions referred to some memory from the camps. "He disguised himself as a Nazi there," I was told by Huber, who had sat at the desk next to his, "and he saved Jews." Sherman remembered that Izbitzky became irritable after an episode involving his daughter. Something sexual the daughter had done at home, a strange thing to tell the guys at the office. "He wanted to kill himself after he saw her naked with this boy"—a memory that lingered, oddly, in the bureau and was tied up with all the dark relations at home. Many years later, when Esther was herself emotionally shattered and close to her death, she would refuse categorically to walk on the street past her childhood home. She wouldn't rent an apartment anywhere near it, treating it as if it were a radioactive fallout zone.

When Esther was four, her brother Ze'ev was born. He was a beautiful child with chiseled features, very fair, and with a slight exotic slant to his eyes, whose gaze was always scrutinizing and arrogant. A kindergarten classmate who would later become a cardiac surgeon remembered Ze'ev as a violent child, the son of an imposing bureaucrat and a mother as meek as a shadow. All of them lived in a dim ground-floor apartment, a place stuffed with heavy furniture, vitrines filled with porcelain, white doilies on every surface. The boy, Ze'ev, exceptionally good-looking, blossomed in that apartment like a tropical plant in the soil of a sooty garden. It was the home of Holocaust survivors, where nothing was spontaneous and everything was twisted and closed off, inhibited and repressed.

In the autumn of 1963, when Ze'ev was eleven years old, his father appeared as a witness for the defense in the Tel Aviv District Court. It was the trial of the orchestra conductor Hirsch Barenblatt, who stood accused of having collaborated with the Nazis while serving as chief of the Jewish police in the Bendzin Ghetto. Barenblatt, who now lives in Germany, was found guilty at the time and sentenced to five years' imprisonment but his conviction was overturned a year later in the Supreme Court. When Izbitzky testified, Bendzin survivors packed the courtroom and twittered like a hatchery. They were divided between those who viewed Barenblatt as a scoundrel who had turned in Jewish orphans and those who saw him as a savior who had assisted the Jewish underground resistance. "Mr. Izbitzky's testimony was confused," the judges wrote in their opinion. "It contains internal contradictions, and contradicts his testimony to the police, and thus cannot be considered reliable."

It took courage to testify on behalf of a man who

symbolized the most reviled and hidden part of the Holocaust. At that time, eighteen years after the war, kapos and Nazi collaborators were still being caught. About sixty Jews who had come to live in Israel were identified by other survivors who remembered the atrocities they had committed. When Izbitzky decided to testify in defense of Barenblatt, whom he also knew well in Israel, one of his neighbors from across the way asked him, "What good can it possibly do you to testify?" He responded: "You can't imagine what went on there. You wanted to save your sister and you shoved someone else to his death in her place."

Many years after the trial, his daughter, Esther, approached a playwright and suggested that together they write a play about her father. They met for several months but nothing came of it. She advanced and retreated, frightened of her own boldness in touching something inside that was liable, by being exposed, to cause her great pain. Yet to leave it in the dark would be devastating, too. She had the transcripts of the trial, and she spoke of the symphony conductor, Barenblatt, and her father as a strange couple connected by a nightmare. To a girl of fifteen, as she was at the time of the trial, the conductor who had worked with the Nazis, deciding who would be sent to the gas chambers, seemed intriguing, illicitly seductive, whereas her father was the opposite: a small, weak, obsessive man who screamed horribly at home and afterwards regretted it. Perhaps it was a forbidden sexual attraction to Satan, coupled with contempt for the weak. But it could have been that for her these were two parts of the same man.

———

Ze'ev heard talk about the trial and his father's testimony at home and on the street. At school he was often ostracized for other reasons. He drew fire and provoked anger in the other kids because he was haughty and rebellious and violent, yet also extremely vulnerable. Once they took his new bike and dropped it into a lime pit. Absolute quiet pervaded the Izbitzky home when Ze'ev came home after the ruckus of school and the street. Silence was imposed in the apartment when the father returned from the office. The frightened mother kept the place absolutely still, like a dog at the door to his master's house. If the quiet was disturbed, the father—a slight, balding man—would pull out his belt with a practiced movement and beat Ze'ev. The neighbor remembers loud shouts and cursing and blows. Once the husband of one of Shula's sisters came to warn Izbitzky to restrain himself because he might hurt someone. The father was the dark center of the house, bearing within him an unresolved something that haunted him. He found an outlet in anger and beatings he would later regret, and then repeat.

As a kind of haven for his soul, the boy, Ze'ev, built himself an imaginary world in which he presided as dream prince, stockpiling huge amounts of information and contriving dreams of grandeur. Only in high school would these link up with the books of Ayn Rand and the extremist philosophy of Moshe Kroy, an individualism that left no room for compassion or closeness. When I consider how Ze'ev ended up, I tend to believe that the groundwork for the bubble that would suffocate him far away from Ben-Yehuda Street was laid in that gloomy ground floor, between the screams and the silences. He and his sister would die within two months of each other, in the same winter, both of them in awful conditions of cold and loneliness, poverty and despair, like the inmates of a concentration camp for whom liberation came too late.

But in that childhood time, when no one had yet conceived of the brutal end, the north of the city of Tel Aviv was a kids' kingdom that lay between two schools. To the west was the sea, with its wild beaches and the rocky cliffs where we searched for secret caves and the abandoned Muslim cemetery with its gaping graves and skulls of the dead. To the east were small lanes paved with limestone gravel. There was a farm overgrown with bushes and trees, a youth-movement cabin, and sooty campfire sites. On a hill by Dizengoff Street rose the Tnuva Restaurant and the Beit Ha-Ofeh Bakery. Between all these was a huge area of sheds, rusty and blackened from the fumes of the Dan garage with its clock tower and bus-shaped gate. To the sides, like rivers, stretched boulevards of trees where we sat high on the backs of benches with our feet on the seats. When we weren't running around outside we were at home, where most of our parents lived modestly, sleeping on a sofa that they opened into a bed each night in the living room. They wanted their children to live better than they did, to succeed where devastation had cut off their own lives.

At first, being strange gave Ze'ev power; later it

hurt him. The kids discovered that there was weakness behind the arrogance. Only in high school did he become big and strong, working hard to build up his body. He was charismatic with the group of new friends that surrounded him, contemptuous of the authority of teachers and of all those who worked like ants for their miserable livelihoods. His physical strength was meant to defend him from violence, to keep his father from raising his hand against him. Those who knew him in high school remember a father different from the one of his childhood years. Avraham was by that time old and sickly and never stopped checking his blood pressure. Now he obtained his after-work silence by means of his weakness. No one was allowed to disturb him because he might get sick. His voice thinned, but Ze'ev was now out of his reach. Neighbors would line up at the entrance to the apartment when Izbitzky checked people's blood pressure, a kind of peculiar hobby. He would listen, hushed and mute, to the sound of blood, as if hearing voices from somewhere.

Ze'ev's sister, after completing her military service, began a career as an avant-garde theater director who would in later years find more success in Denmark, Boston, and Harlem than in Israel. Expectations were also high for Ze'ev. He had a light-haired, pretty girlfriend who remembers, as do all his friends, that Ze'ev was the boy with a destiny. Great things were expected of him. Maybe because he was smart, full of charm and fire, radiated something that was different, and knew he would be an architect. Sometimes he would sketch plans for huge buildings on his desk during classes, drawings that hung over the top of the desk down to the floor. He once helped a band of students steal a chemistry exam and invented a clever method of copying during tests that was still in use years later. Its centerpiece was the preparation of long, narrow strips of paper on which the material being tested was recorded. The strips were slipped into one's socks in a precise order, which was recorded in code on the desk. The crib sheets could then be accessed unobtrusively while the student's eyes remained on the exam. Ze'ev had a very strange style of handwriting, different from everybody else's.

Girls liked Izbitzky and he was drawn to them everywhere as if haunted by their scent, but he never established any deep emotional ties. He always stood alone, egocentric and hungry for challenges, clench-fisted, a schemer who toyed with life and entertained himself with his ability to persuade everyone of the most ridiculous things. He was confident in the power of his mind and saw the world lying at his feet, full of infinite possibilities. Who thought then about what it had been like to live as Ze'ev had in his childhood, what living in a house of Holocaust survivors, between a short-tempered father and ostracizing classmates, had done to him. Who knew how deep the scars went into his soul.

The twenty-five years since high school spin but a short story. The details are few and so are the witnesses, and from a certain point onward—when the time arrived for the great promise to be realized—everything goes foggy and there are no witnesses at all.

After graduating, Ze'ev went to the army's pilots' course, but didn't make the cut. Lichtenstein, his friend from school, ran into him in armored corps basic training in Rafiah, running through the sand until his breath was gone and freezing in the guard tower. Within a year Ze'ev was commander of a tank whose job it was to bridge trenches so that other tanks could cross them. During an incursion into Lebanon his tank got stuck in a deep ditch and held up the entire army behind him for hours. A year later the war of 1973 crashed down on him, and Lichtenstein heard at some point that all the trench-bridgers had been destroyed at the Suez Canal. He mourned Ze'ev as if he were dead. But afterwards he saw him, whole and healthy, and thought to himself how Ze'ev always survived any ordeal.

After his army service Ze'ev studied economics for a year at the university. But he was soon fed up with school. Ayn Rand and the rebellion of the giants and all the promises of conquering the world filled him with impatience and led him far from home. He was in India and Tibet when his sister married her lover, the son of the diamond magnate Herbst. She took luxury trips to the Riviera and then to Manhattan, realizing the Polish dream of wealth and champagne, and enrolling in New York University. Ze'ev returned from Tibet only when he heard that his father had died. Izbitzky of the dues bureau had been defeated by his high blood pressure. A short film made by a friend remains from that visit of mourning; in it Ze'ev appears as a tall young man with long hair and a mustache, dressed in a winter coat, his gaze passing beyond and disappearing somewhere over the cameraman's shoulder. Ze'ev himself toyed with enigmatic still photography, peering at bathers on the beach.

After sitting *shiva* for his father, he hopped over to New York. His sister lived there with her husband in a dream apartment in the heart of Manhattan. She was a favorite of the theater department and directed *Mr. Slick* in a spine-tingling production that won much praise. As a result of that trip, Ze'ev remained in New York for twenty years, until his end, returning to Israel only every few years for a short visit. He was in a rush to either get away from the world or conquer it, his friends said, caught up in his dream of robust individualism, without compassion, living a loneliness that could sear an entire continent. Even when his sister separated from her husband, when she discovered her lesbian inclinations and returned to Israel, Ze'ev remained there. What did he do, his friends sometimes wondered? His mother said that Zevik was working on a large and secret research project. He was seeking, for mankind, a cure for cancer, and, for the Mafia, the mathematical formula that would break Las Vegas's casinos.

Something about him always drove friends to seek him out, yet at the same time prevented them from finding him. One friend met him in the Village in New York in a line for a performance by Merce Cunningham, but his good friend Schwartz lived in New York for three years and never ran into him at all. When someone did arrive in New York and spoke with him, Ze'ev preferred to meet on the street or in a café. He guarded the secret of his apartment zealously, speaking only of a Chinese woman who lived with him and took care of him, and of his great research project that the world would someday be worthy of receiving.

In the muddy winter that followed the Lebanon War, in 1982, he suddenly showed up in Israel in his army uniform and went to help Ariel Sharon, because he believed that "he's the next great leader who will save the country." He spent forty days in a tank in the land of cherries and then returned to New York. During another visit to Tel Aviv he asked a childhood friend to take him to the street where Semadar, his sweet youthful love, lived. She was already married and had two children. Ten years after graduating, he remembered her and reached out for her memory, forcing his friend to sit with him in a car next to her house half the night, until the lights went out in the apartment window. From time to time his school friends would get together and wonder about Izbitzky. They waited for him to do something big. After all, he'd always bobbed to the surface and gotten by. Someone said he'd set up a moving company. Every rumor stuck because no one knew anything about him.

The only one of his friends to get a peek into the place where Izbitzky lived was Dishi, the film director. Dishi came to New York and went to the address he had, a YMCA on Staten Island. The Y was built in a radial beehive design, like a prison, and when he emerged from the elevator on the ninth floor, Dishi found Ze'ev

in a tiny room alongside the rooms of the unemployed
and social-service cases who lived there by the month.
Ze'ev was still good-looking and strong, as Dishi remembered him. A black-and-white television was suspended
above his head, tuned to the local stations day and
night. A bicycle leaned against a wall, and there was a
sink and faucet and a jar so that he could avoid trips to
the bathroom at the end of the corridor. And there
were lots of books for the great research project. Being
alone was a shield against a world that had no faith in
him. He spoke of a philosophy that would heal the
world's ills. The two friends spent an entire night wandering the streets until their legs ached. In one café
Ze'ev told Dishi, "Look, that woman's hot for you,"
meaning the woman sitting behind him. He was acutely
alert to everything that happened 360 degrees around
him. Awash in his old craving for camaraderie, he interrogated Dishi about the lives of their pals. "In a year or
two you'll know everything," he promised. Dishi noticed
that Ze'ev had developed the habits of a survivor who
lived on a tight budget. He knew about every sale where
you got a hamburger free for every three you bought,
and the little refrigerator in his room was filled with
them—cooked hamburgers wrapped in paper.

The last time he came to Israel was when his mother,
Shula, was dying. She was suffering from Alzheimer's.
He left before she died, and when he didn't show up for
the funeral, his sister, Esther, and his mother's sisters
and his uncles knew that something bad must be happening with him. The death of his mother had cut the

last cord of life. She was the one who would ask friends about Ze'ev, send him letters and money, and maintain ties of concern. When she died, it was as if the anchor that had held him to the place he did not want to be had broken free. He was swept away like a demon-ravaged refugee ship. Esther was living in Boston at the time, working in an old-age home, living in difficult conditions, but never forgetting her brother for a moment. Uncle Tzvi came over from Israel once and together he and Esther climbed to the ninth floor of the Y and tried to persuade Ze'ev to let someone examine him, to accept treatment, to return to Tel Aviv where he could get medical care. His disengagement had become an illness. His rebellious youthful charm had become paranoia. They sat with him in a restaurant and fed him and he talked about the FBI following him, all the while seeming quite coherent and optimistic and refusing to acknowledge that he might be wrong. The more they pushed him to accept help, the more distant he became, and Esther finally gave up. Her heart was broken over her brother. A psychiatrist from Mt. Sinai Hospital, a friend of Esther's, tried to speak to Ze'ev a few times. He tried to arrange to meet him in the flophouse where he had moved after the Y, but Ze'ev refused to see him.

At some point he disappeared. The family didn't have even the beginnings of a clue. He was thrown out of his last residence for not paying his rent. He went on the street and was swallowed up by the megalopolis of millions. When his sister killed herself as the rains began in Tel Aviv, no one knew how to notify him. In

December, two months later, before anyone could get over the shock of her death—she had hung herself from a beam in her rented apartment—the foreign ministry notified relatives that Ze'ev's body had been found in New York. His aunts decided that he should be brought to Israel. No one in the family knew what had finished him. They thought that maybe he had frozen to death on the street. Neither did anyone want to pry too much.

His friends, who still didn't know what had happened, sometimes thought that maybe someone should go rescue him, as if his trail had disappeared in India. But no one went. Some time passed before I managed to find out how his life had ended. I discovered that Ze'ev Izbitzky, who had been born two months before me, in the spring of 1952, had died on December 9, 1994, the very same week that his friend Dishi was filming homeless people in New York for a documentary he was making. The address found on his body was his dead sister's in Boston. Cause of death: suicide. There were two telephone numbers on the death certificate read to me over the phone from New York. One belonged to a man named Ronnie and the other to the Jewish burial-society worker, Mendel, who had taken care of the body. Ronnie was the detective who found Ze'ev; Mendel, the gravedigger, gave me the address of a building on Staten Island. It turned out to be an old-age home.

It was nighttime, afternoon in Staten Island, when I spoke with a man named Markowitz, who held the key to the last year of Ze'ev's life. We spoke for half an hour on a transatlantic line until a heavy silence fell.

According to Markowitz, Ze'ev, the guy whom our neighborhood knew as "God," was thrown out of his last domicile in the winter and became homeless. He froze in the severe cold and was taken to the hospital, where his two feet were amputated. He spent half a year in the hospital fighting treatment, shoving away the life he had already lost interest in, until he was released and transferred to a Jewish old-age home on Staten Island. There, perhaps as a kind of final mercy, he found Markowitz, the home's director, who had once been a soldier in Israel. Ze'ev got around on crutches, wrote things on matchbooks, smoked cigarettes he found, and spoke with Markowitz. No one called him and he didn't write to anyone. He didn't have the papers he had written over the years, he didn't know about his sister's death, and he never said a word about his family or about the real estate that awaited him in Tel Aviv. "Ze'ev," Markowitz told me, "spoke very little about his previous life. I thought that when the time came he would say something, but I didn't pressure him."

On the second Friday of December, in the morning, Ze'ev opened a third-floor window in the old-age home and jumped out. He died immediately. "There was no letter or paper. Just a woman from Brooklyn who called and asked the same questions you're asking now."

THE
PARATROOPER OFFICER'S
PALESTINIAN MOM

FROM WHAT AGE do a person's memories begin? Three years old? Five? Are nebulous images from one's nursing days imprinted in the memory? Benda remembers no mother, no caressing touch, no soft word before sleep. Only a shredded scene of a receding woman, an old man raising a hand to strike, a miserable boy standing in the center of a large yard. Everything else is information—some of it literally intelligence—that he himself has collected about his life, piece by piece, many years after the fact, after he'd already been a wild child, stealing to live, and then a wagon driver's helper, a paratrooper, an audacious commander of retaliation raids against Palestinian terrorist bases, an agent of the Shin Bet, Israel's secret security agency, and a businessman whose line was protecting gold mines, Jewish communities, and film stars.

Benda knew that he had been born in the winter of '38 in Shabazi, a Jewish neighborhood in Tel Aviv very close to the sea, and to the Arab neighborhood of Manshiyya. The street is still there, a line of squat, shabby houses at the end of the renovated Neve Tzedek quarter. He knew that his father, who had been called Moshe Ben-David, had escaped alone from Yemen. Here, in Israel, he had married Margalit, who had immigrated as a girl with her family from Iraq in a caravan that had crossed through Transjordan. Only years later did Benda discover what his vanished parents looked like, when he looked at old photographs and saw a man and woman who were, to him, total strangers. He remembered a scene from the house on Zerach Brant Street in which his grandfather, Yochanan, raised his hand against a young woman. A fuzzy picture of violence, with Benda, a small boy, watching from the side. There was also a small and quiet grandmother, diffident as a shadow. His parents were very young, really just teenagers. Then something happened, and the next picture seared into Benda's memory is the orphanage. He stands in a courtyard, a four-year-old surrounded by taunting boys. Absent from the picture is a mother to place a comforting hand on his shoulder. There is no one but the boys. "And I stand at attention and am very angry about something, perhaps about them having left me." From that moment, he was alone there, in that old building, for four years. An ultraorthodox orphanage leached of compassion and love, with only beatings and Torah. What happened to bring him there? Who abandoned him there? For years he was told that his father had been killed fighting with the British somewhere in Europe during World War II and that his mother had died in an Egyptian bombing raid on the Central Bus Station in Tel Aviv. That was the family story. There were no graves to confirm it.

My meetings with Benda, which culminated in a journey into the past, were conducted in a small restaurant near the diamond exchange, where some of his old secret-agent buddies ran security firms. It was the first time he ever told his story to a stranger. He had held it inside him for so many years, and even his closest friends knew nothing about it. But at the age of fifty-seven, when his success was assured and his life was in order—children, grandchildren, business—he paused to return to the past. It takes strength to go back to the dark places where one's life lies buried without a gravestone. When Benda spoke of his life, I felt the little boy from the orphanage, David Ben-David, materializing beside us, gazing in wonder at the image of himself as an adult—Benda.

"Fifteen years ago I went back to the orphanage and walked around without saying who I was. I saw that there were still orphans like me, and in the offices they remembered a Ben-David who'd been a wild kid. They took out my file, but it didn't even have the name of the person who brought me. There was only a letter from the orphanage headmaster to Agudat Yisrael, the ultra-orthodox organization that sponsored the facility, saying that he could not be responsible for the life of this wild boy Ben-David if they did not build a wall around the institution."

He was a tough little guy who quickly learned how to defend himself and his honor and became a member of a gang of kids that ruled the yard under the command of the orphan Hazan. That enabled him to grab the best clothes from the pile that was thrown out into the center of the yard every Friday after the washing. They prayed and studied only Torah, embroidery, and how to work in the vegetable garden. Anyone who got a teacher angry was beaten by the headmaster, who once even broke Benda's hand when he refused to tell on another boy. They played and ran, were forced to pray, and were very frightened. Relatives came to visit only on weekends.

There is still a photograph that shows a six-year-old Benda with three women who later turned out to be his mother and her sisters. But he remembers himself always playing alone during the visits, under the big *domim* tree in the corner of the yard. A ragpicker was often hunched there, next to an old shed filled with broken things. "As a lonely boy, I made friends with the old man, and it was only years later that I realized he'd been my grandfather, my mother's father. The two of us would talk the way an old man talks with a boy. If he knew I was his grandson, why didn't he tell me? I feel a great anger about him being there and not talking to me about me."

If Benda is angry, you can't see it in his face. He's a tall and impressive man, very dark, wiry, his face narrow, his nose like an eagle's beak. His eyes scrutinize you but divulge nothing about their master. He's taut, reticent, yet displays the warm and easygoing nature of a senior officer for whom the military has been a family and whose army comrades have been his brothers and sisters. He speaks with them on his cell phone with an affection reserved for the closest of friends. At some of our meetings he was joined by one of them, also a veteran of the Shin Bet, demonstrating exactly how far the boy Ben-David had come from standing alone in the yard of the Agudat Yisrael orphanage, and what a long road he traveled from there into the sheltered core of the Israeli security community.

When he was eight years old Ben-David ran away from the orphanage and never went back. On the street he met two other abandoned boys, Schlessinger, an orphan who'd come to Israel alone from the Holocaust, and Tadri, and they formed their own little gang. This was his first family in years. They sold newspapers on the street, ate discarded remains of falafel sandwiches, cleaned the Beit Ha-Am Cinema after the last show, smoked cigarette butts, lugged wet clothes from the laundry to customers' homes, hauled heavy blocks of ice to upper stories, and at night slept huddled together in the back of the iceman's wagon.

In exchange for a place to sleep in a stable on the outskirts of Tel Aviv, the boys would wake up twice a night and lead the horses to their feed and water. They stood much lower than the horses and they had to turn them carefully to lead them to the trough. Sometimes they got a hoof in the face and fell, stunned, onto the straw. Benda eventually advanced to the rank of assistant to the wagon driver, Glick, who would sometimes, out of compassion, take him home. There he could wash himself, eat a home-cooked meal, and sleep comfortably on a bed they made up for him in the bathtub.

"I didn't turn into a real criminal," Benda told me, "only a petty thief, to feed myself. We swiped clothes drying on lines, and wallets, or food left out by old people drowsing in their apartments." Now and then older burglars would hoist them up to small windows so that they could get into a store and open it from the inside. Once Benda was sent into a corner grocery and knocked down all the shelves as he clambered in. He was caught by a British policeman but freed a few hours later because he was only nine or ten years old. Gaunt from hunger and quick as an alley cat, he would wander the prosperous parts of Tel Aviv on Saturdays with Tadri and Schlessinger to inhale the aroma of the Sabbath *tsholent* stew wafting from the homes. They hunted pigeons in the sycamore trees of King George Street near the ice factory and fried them up together with vegetables they lifted from the market. There was a great sense of camaraderie among them. David, Schlessinger from the Holocaust, and Tadri against the whole world, and against other gangs that fought for their livelihoods on the same turf.

When David was ten years old, Egyptian planes swooped down over Tel Aviv and he hawked newspapers right and left under fire. But that night people came to the stables, woke up the homeless boys, and dragged them to a house surrounded by a new fence in the Nachalat Yitzchak neighborhood. At the gate was a sign: "Secure Institution for Juvenile Delinquents." That's how Benda first learned what he was. "Goons grabbed me, stripped me, and scrubbed me with stiff brushes. They gave us a blue uniform and work shoes."

He quickly adjusted to the new place. When you've got no one to turn and plead to and no one to expect any help from, you manage. There was a teacher there who organized a group of abandoned kids to go to a kibbutz. The teacher took notice of Benda, cultivated him, taught him about the world outside the institution, and then sent him to Kibbutz Ein Shemer—a warm, shielding paradise where Pino and Perele adopted him as their son. Suddenly he had a home, after years of drifting like a street dog without anyone in the world.

Even then he was a boy who knew nothing about his past, and there was no one who could tell him. At the kibbutz, when adolescence stirred up questions of identity, Benda began wondering where he came from. He went a few times to the house on Zerach Brant Street to meet his mother's family and hear what had happened to him in childhood. "They stuck to the story that the mother had been killed at the Central Bus Station, one of the dozens of victims of the bombing raid. But there was always someone off on the side who said that maybe she hadn't died. So I suspected that there was a secret being hidden from me."

When he was sixteen Benda decided he wanted to

be a paratrooper. Those were the years before the Sinai Campaign of 1956, the years when Palestinian fedayeen crossed the borders to carry out terrorist attacks on Israel and the Israeli army crossed back on retaliation raids. An aura surrounded the paratrooper commanders of the retaliation units—people like Arik Sharon, Motta Gur, Meir Har-Tzion, and Raful—who could sometimes be seen around the kibbutz or in the dining hall, their special uniforms dusty and sandy. "I wanted so badly to belong to that elite brotherhood, to be someone, so I went to the paratroopers' enlistment cabin. The legendary Marcel Tubias was the one who saw me there—I was a sixteen-year-old kid, tall and slight— and I told him that my father had been killed as a soldier in the British army's Jewish Brigade." Perhaps that tipped the scales in his favor, for the paratroop brigade was also a refuge for outsiders of exceptional courage who could hold up in the unit—in part because they had no place to return to and nothing to lose. "I was a boy soldier and I loved the army. Water rationing on forced marches never bothered me. I really loved being part of that bold team on its long hikes, alerts, maneuvers, and retaliation raids."

Here, all at once, the orphan Benda, the boy without a past, was part of a fellowship of fighters, a society unrivaled for providing a sense of home. It offers passion and pride, glory and honor, and especially belonging, everything that a man who has nothing needs to pick himself up from the gutter and become someone of value. It didn't take long for his name to get around and to appear here and there in stories of paratrooper valor. He and his comrades raided Kuntila and Sabha, took Syrian officers prisoner in the north, and went on missions on the Syrian shore of the Sea of Galilee. His nearest brush with death actually came, however, when he was serving as an instructor in a parachuting course. He was jumping from a Dakota after his men and his parachute got caught on the aircraft's tail—the horizontal stabilizer. He was dragged helplessly behind the plane, buffeted brutally by the wind, until his friend the jump master, who remained inside, spotted a black lump trailing behind the plane. Together with several other men, he managed, after great exertions, to pull Benda in. They saved him from being smeared on the runway just minutes before the plane had to land.

At around that same time, Benda received an indication from someone that his mother had not been killed in the war, that she was living in Lod or Ramla. He went there and looked for a woman named Margalit, but found nothing.

Benda's greatest desire was to become a paratroop officer. But he was already married to a girl from the kibbutz and had a daughter, so his requests for officers' school were rejected time and again. Until one Saturday when he remained at base as company master sergeant and an alert came saying that the Syrians had crossed the border. Benda sent a machine-gun detachment alongside a narrow canal near the Dardara marshes to cover his flank as he drove on ahead. It was too late when he saw a Syrian soldier standing, beside other soldiers kneeling, all aiming their weapons at the Israeli squad. The Syrian ambush shot a volley of fire that grazed Benda and killed the man next to him in the patrol car.

The machine-gun detachment returned fire and the entire sector ignited. Bullets blazed for three hours and the patrol car was stuck, with two men dead and three wounded. With the exception of Benda and another soldier, none of the men were in any condition to move from the site of the attack. So Benda extricated the wounded, saving their lives, and in the process became a hero. He was immediately sent to officers' school and began to climb the ladder in Paratroop Brigade 50, until he became a company commander, leading his men on raids and incursions over the border, blowing up Arab police stations, and doing reconnaissance work. He was a strict and stubborn officer who accepted no compromises, the sort who never speaks about his past, not even to his fellow officers. Often, when on a mission behind enemy lines in Syria or Jordan, Benda would find himself overwhelmed by the thought that if he were killed there would be no mother to mourn him.

Before discovering his past, Benda almost died again, for the third time in his life. On the sixth of June in '67, when he was twenty-nine years old, on the night of the first day of the Six Day War, he stood in the front of his halftrack, leading his troops in the battle at the Rafiah outposts. An antitank round hit his vehicle. The shell killed the gunner at his side and shattered Benda's right leg. Everything was on fire, and they lay there together, a huge pile of Batallion 50 wounded, on the sand dunes at Rafiah. The battalion halted. Egyptian mortar shells fell around them. He spent half a year with a smashed leg, with fractures and advancing gangrene, going from one hospital to another. In the end the leg had to be amputated below the knee. In an old newspaper I found a piece about Benda the one-legged paratrooper insisting on making a jump onto the beach at Ashdod. The street urchin was now one of the heroes of the immigrant state.

After he and his first wife divorced, he married Noa from Kibbutz Hatzor. Now the father of three, he was once more devoid of a past, as if he had begun his life at the kibbutz. Yet sometimes that strange feeling came over him, the one he found no explanation for. When we sat together he told me that it happened, of all times, whenever he crossed the border with his men on a retaliation raid into Jordan. Then, he felt, as with a boy's intuition, that he'd been deceived when they told him his mother was dead. It seemed to him that if he would invest just a fraction of his military energy into finding out the truth about his past, he could resolve the mystery of his life. But each time he got close, he withdrew, retreated. The urge to find out was great, but not as great as his fear of poking at a wound that threatened to bleed uncontrollably. That is how I felt, too, during my encounters with him, and when we later crossed the border into Jordan.

After his injury he was deep into carving out a new niche for himself in the military. An officer who's missing a leg is not destined for a great combat career, but Benda stuck with the army and rose to chief of the Special Operations Branch. This was the period of missions along the Gulf of Suez—such as Israel's nabbing of an Egyptian radar station and the occupation of Green Island—joint operations involving boats and engineer units and navy commandos. Following a senior command course he was sent to head the IDF jump school, returning with one foot to the place his life had almost ended when he'd been towed behind that Dakota. He always loved the uncertainty in parachuting, the fear, and the defeat of the fear that overpowers you when you step out of the aircraft and plummet dizzily to the ground.

Everything that had been hidden from him for years suddenly descended on him when he was thirty-six and serving as military governor of Jericho. The silence broke in an instant. Benda hadn't wanted the position. He had wanted to advance in combat operations, but with one leg there was no hope of that. After three and a half years as commander of the jump school, where every kid who wanted a red beret had jumped under him, he was named to be sent to South America as a military attaché. But that appointment didn't work out and in its place he was offered the job of military governor of the Jericho district with command of the bridges over the Jordan. It was as if a cunning theater director were preparing the stage for the next scene.

Benda had resisted the appointment but ultimately caved in to the pressure and went down to Jericho. He even learned to enjoy himself there. He was a relatively liberal governor who built a Peace Park for the city's children and maintained good relations with Mayor Shafiq Bali. One day his uncle from Shabazi, his mother's brother, called and said that two strangers had been wandering around Zerach Brant Street near his home asking about his grandmother—the mother of his dead mother, Margalit, who had died twenty-six years ago. Why would anyone be looking for the old woman, Benda wondered. The two people, the uncle reported, had told him that Margalit was alive. In Jordan. Married, and a mother, with relatives in Nablus.

Thus did the dead mother rise from her graveless past, the mother whose face Benda remembered only blurrily and whose touch he recalled not at all. He was astonished, and yet the revelation fit with some inexplicable feeling buried inside him—the abandoned orphan's hope that one day it would turn out that his mother was alive. He was in just the right place to find out whether the story was true, and he approached the task in the way he was most accustomed to—as a military man. With the help of Shin Bet commander Yitzhak Tzur he began to make inquiries. He sent out advance patrols, people who went through Amman, looking around, keeping their eyes open. Antennas were raised and material accumulated. Photographs of the woman arrived, along with her address and the names of her children. It was professional military espionage—in search of a mother. Finally someone inquired of her whether she would like to visit the family in Shabazi that she had not seen for so many years. They sent her snapshots of her Israeli family to encourage her to cross the bridges, and overcome her fear that they were setting a trap for her after she had moved to an enemy country. She very much wanted to visit and received assurances that nothing bad would be done to her. From his seat in Jericho, Benda wove a thick web to snag what had eluded him for so many years.

The mother who he'd been told for years was dead crossed the Allenby Bridge on a fierce summer morning in 1974. As she reached the frisking station at the border, Benda was watching her from a concealed position. He saw an older woman, a Palestinian husband, and a girl having their passports stamped, then being examined. Afterwards he drove quickly to his office on the second floor of the garrison building at Camp Hanan and waited. Earlier in the day the office had been scrubbed and polished as never before. The governor's uniform and his officer's insignia also sparkled. The Jordanian woman was brought into the room with her husband and daughter. A taxi had brought them there from the bridge. Terrified, not comprehending what was happening, they were directed into the office of the military governor, which in Jordan, too, is a fear-inducing title.

When Benda described the encounter to me, it sounded like a formal interrogation. Which is precisely what he intended. He'd sought to turn the tables on his abandonment so many years ago. Now, in his office, the life and safety of his mother were in his hands—to condemn or to pardon. From the other side of his desk he began, with the help of an interpreter, to interrogate the

Jordanian woman about her life and family. He believed that a military-style interrogation would yield the sort of details he would not be able to get once his identity was revealed. "It's known to us that you were born a Jew," he told her. "You moved there with an Arab in '48, correct? Tell me everything. We know also that you left a boy here. Do you know what became of him? How old was he when you left?"

"I kept myself composed," Benda told me as we sat in the restaurant at the diamond exchange. "But the interpreter, who knew the whole story, started to cry. I shouted at him in Hebrew to be quiet, not to cry. I sat facing her, my uniform ironed, everything in the room sparkling. I wanted to create a strong contrast between now and the past—between her abandoning me to an orphanage and my success in getting out of there. Not to be vengeful . . . no. But it was a one-time opportunity that had suddenly come to the people who had played in this drama thirty years before. . . . Here she was, sitting apprehensively, being interrogated, with no idea who the man facing her was. I wanted to create a situation such that when she heard who I was, it would have the strongest possible effect. Yes, it was a reversal. Now she was the weak orphan."

The details flowed from the woman, creating a partial picture of her life. She didn't say everything there, but it came out that she had been declared dead by her father, and the rest of her family, for having left her Jewish husband—the oud-player Moshe, David's father. She left and followed an Arab boy she had met in the adjacent neighborhood, Manshiyya, to his home in Lydda. She married him and bore him children. Then she left him as well and married his brother, and in the great flight of '48, when the Arabs of Lydda were expelled, she fled with them, sharing the fate of the Palestinians. She escaped to Jordan, where she put down roots. She spoke with Benda while her worried husband sat next to her and the girl huddled close to them.

He asked her one last question, whether she would like to see her son. "That's why I'm here," she answered in Arabic, having forgotten all her Hebrew. "So I stood up and told her, 'Here is your son, here, in front of you.' And she came to me and hugged me and kissed me and cried a great deal, and both of them, her husband, too, kissed me and cried, and she said, 'For an instant I thought it was you, because of your left eyebrow that slants upwards.' But I didn't cry," Benda told me. "I'm not built for having a mother, for an older woman to be hugging me. Now I knew that she was in fact my mother, but I had grown up without her. All my life she was missing for me, and I was always falling in love with teachers and counselors. . . . To this day I have a special connection with women, but you can't suddenly get a mother in the middle of your life. You just can't."

He took his mother and her husband and their daughter from Jericho to a hotel in Tel Aviv, and that same evening they all went to see the grandmother in Shabazi. All her brothers came. They hadn't seen her since she was banned from their home as a dead woman, and now "there was a great shedding of tears." But she kept her composure—a strong woman who had had a difficult life of desertions and wanderings, and who had known how to hide things for so many years. For three days he traveled the country with them, to all the sites of the Land of Israel, of the old Palestine, Acre and Jaffa, Ramla and Lod, as Lydda was now called, places they knew from the old country that had already been covered by the new. The senior Israeli officer and his mother, her Palestinian husband and their little girl, who did not move from her mother, and who would be killed ten years later in a traffic accident in Amman. Benda listened and said nothing of what had happened to him all those years. They parted in a café in Jerusalem, and when his mother's husband asked what would happen if they wanted to come live there. "Come," Benda told them, and the words remained suspended in the air of the coffeehouse.

Then nothing for twenty years. Not a word was exchanged. "And I wasn't satisfied, for I hadn't managed to get down to the truth, to what had really happened between her and me as a boy. Even during that interrogation she hadn't told the truth. She was scared."

For twenty years there was silence, as if a stifling blanket had once again been thrown over the words that were not to be spoken. The army did not discharge him when the matter of his mother became known. Benda left the army of his own accord. But prior to that he had gone to Chief of Staff Motta Gur so that the latter might decide what should be done with an officer whose mother is a citizen of an enemy state. In the chief of staff's office Benda laid his past on the table, and there it sat, like a loaded pistol. But Motta, who had a warm spot in his heart for his paratroopers, sat with him for two hours and promised him that he'd suffer no harm. Benda had been military governor of Jericho for a year, and if he wished to leave that post, the Shin Bet was looking for a senior army man.

In the autumn of 1975 he went for an interview with the Shin Bet chief, Avrom Shalom. Benda told him he had something to relate that he hoped would not be an obstacle to being accepted by that agency. When Benda finished talking, the chief removed his glasses, rubbed his weary eyes, and said: I actually think it will be an obstacle. "I was very angry," Benda told me, "because I was not willing for the past to stop me, after I had extricated myself from it with such difficulty. It shouldn't determine what security clearance I get."

We'll be in touch with you, the Shin Bet chief said to him. Immediately Benda chased down his friends, who didn't know anything about the matter—he'd only told his wife, Noa—and asked them to help out, to do what they could to help his case. A year after meeting his mother in Jericho he was accepted into the Shin Bet. For six years he moved from country to country, running around the world protecting embassies from Palestinian terrorism. He proved an extremely demanding boss, who handed out Amos Elon's biography of Herzl to his men and who allowed no half-measures.

While working at an embassy in Asia, he bought a stereo system so elaborate that colleagues asked why he

had purchased such expensive equipment. He responded
that as a boy, when he foraged for food in people's back-
yards, he'd listen to the music coming out of the houses.
He had sworn then that one day he'd have music like
that in his own home.

A short time before the Lebanon War began he
retired and went home. During the war, however, with
mines exploding around supply convoys, he volun-
teered for another six months of active service. After
that he took some time off, until a telephone call came
from a Filipino millionaire who was staying at the Tel
Aviv Hilton and sought Benda's advice about the protection of his business interests. Benda flew to the
Philippines for a month and ended up staying for three
years. With seven Israelis working under him, he set up
security systems for Philippine farms and trained body-
guards. In the jungles of Mindanao, the southern island
that swarmed with bandits and underground movements, Benda set up a procedure for transporting gold
safely from the mines. Until his arrival, it had been
stolen almost weekly during its trek through the jun-
gle. He built guard posts equipped with spotlights,
machine guns, and armed men, and operated cargo
planes and electronic detection systems.

His name surfaced twice in the Israeli press in this
period. Once was when a mercenary who had worked
for him told reporters that Benda was a thief and
squealer. Another time it was in connection with Colom-
bian drug lords. In both cases he came out clean. "An
acclaimed one-legged fighter," was how one newspaper

referred to him. "When he was offered half a million dollars to install a security system in the home of the head of one of Colombia's drug cartels, he refused, because he sensed who his client was."

After the Philippines he went on to Miami, where he has now lived for years, running an international security business. Exactly twenty years had passed since the farewell in a Jerusalem café before he once again communicated with his mother and her family, "and in those twenty years there was nothing, zilch."

When his mother's sons began calling from Jordan during the winter after the signing of the Israel-Jordan peace treaty, he asked them why they hadn't been in touch for twenty years, why they hadn't come back for a visit. After all, they'd discovered that Israel was not vicious. They said that their father had been scared and wouldn't allow it. After he died, the time was right. Together they arranged that Benda would call the mother's house when the entire family was sitting around the table. When they picked up the phone on the other side, on a line opened after peace came, he heard shouts: *David, David, David.* "I spoke with everyone, with all my brothers and sisters, *hamdilla*, God bless them," he told me and laughed, his face glowing as if he'd found a secret treasure. Five brothers and two sisters. "They wanted to come, and I said no, first *I'll* come, I'll see them at their home base. Maybe now, when there's peace, and my mother is surrounded by her sons, the truth will come out, she won't be afraid like she had been in Jericho."

"What truth are you still seeking?" I ask him. "Why she abandoned you?"

———

"I won't put it like that. . . . She's not on trial. . . . I simply want to know why she left me, what made her leave, how a mother leaves her two-year-old son and goes away. After all, there's a mother's animal instinct. I'll ask if it bothered her that she left me, if she took any interest in me."

In December 1994, Benda sent a fax to his brother's factory in Amman, and during the third week in March he crossed the northern Sheikh Hussein Bridge near Kibbutz Ashdot Ya'akov on his way to see his new family. I was at his side. The air was fragrant with spring blossoms, the hills green and covered with high grass that hid the machine-gun positions and the Jordan Valley outposts. Beyond the iron gate on the Jordanian side, Colonel 'Az e-Din came up to greet Benda. The Jordanians knew what was going on. Everything had been arranged so as not to harm the mother or her family, and to ensure that no shadow of suspicion fell over them. The desert kingdom is a land in which the secret police watch everything, and military roadblocks preserve a delicate balance, protecting the country from slipping back into the chaos of September 1970.

We sat a long while in the VIP cabin, speaking about the folly of war. Where tourists now haggled over the price of a rental car, there had once been an army position where soldiers were shot and killed. "Who telephoned my mother to notify her that I'm coming?" Benda asked, and the Jordanian colonel said that he had called. In the other room, on an army cot, a Jordanian plainclothes security man dismantled a gold-colored 9-mm pistol. A yellow cab loaded up our luggage and began the climb up the mountain. For Benda, each road sign recalled an Israeli retaliation raid against Jordan from his paratrooper days. The sites were like the names of targets on an intelligence map. Near Shuna, Benda said, "Here we crossed the river at night, and an officer drowned in the strong current." Then came Um Qa'is and Irbid and Zarka and Jarash. That same week Jordan was celebrating the twenty-seventh anniversary of its victory over Israel in the bloody battle at Karameh.

At intervals, a view of nearby Israel spread below our feet—the edge of the Sea of Galilee and Tiberias and Beit Gavriel, and an Egged bus straining up the slope above El-Hama. We passed the Ghur Canal and a small military roadblock where they checked passports. "It's strange to be coming through here without a gun," Benda said. He was moved, but his face remained expressionless. He was worried the whole time that they might steal the luggage, that someone from the past might identify him. The echo of a hidden drum came back at us from the mountain, like an ardent inner beat. It was only when we reached the edge of Amman, on the wide road, that Benda sighed: "Fifty-four years coming to a close."

The rooms of the Forte Grande Hotel were comfortable and looked out over the seven hills of bright Amman. After some hours passed and it began to grow dark, the phone in Benda's room rang. His brothers and sisters were waiting downstairs. From the elevator, Benda was able to identify them all from the snapshots they had sent. One of them, the second brother, born in 1944 in Lydda, looked like Benda's double, tall and dark, with a narrow face like his.

We drove to the mother's house in two cars, going down well-lit streets, past a small amusement park with a Ferris wheel. We saw photographs of King Hussein on bridges and gates; we saw huge public squares and broad avenues. At the windows of the apartment, on the second floor, people were standing, waving their hands, as if a large parade were going by. His mother stood at the door. A dark, elderly woman in a purple dress interwoven with gold. "Oy," she said, falling on his shoulder. She kissed and hugged him, and the family applauded. There was a crowd there, because the orphan had returned to the bosom of his huge family. They stood in a long line to kiss him. Old people and children, babies in their mothers' arms and boys with a trace of a mustache. "For fifty years I haven't seen you," his mother told him, as if the visit to Jericho had never been.

They walked, locked in an embrace, until they landed on a couch in the parlor, and the two identical brothers—Benda and his twin—sat on either side of the mother, like the two dark wings of a golden butterfly. Above their heads I saw a drawing of the deceased daughter. Other members of the family watched from the side, from adjacent rooms, some of them frightened or apprehensive, some alienated by the bomb that had just landed on the house—the lost brother, an enemy officer, and who knows what this will do to us.

When they discovered that there was also a journalist in the house, they were afraid of a reaction from Hamas and asked that their names be changed. Despite that, they exulted in their mother's joy. The story was like a game of dice, with a new face turning up at each roll. Were they Palestinians dreaming of returning to plundered Jaffa, or brothers? Enemies from the evil past, or friends of the new peace? Antagonists or comrades? They were mulling both the opportunities and the dangers. "How are you? What do you want to eat?" the mother suddenly blurted out in Hebrew, recalling a few ancient sentences that had been forgotten during all those years when she had hidden her origins.

Benda's hand rested on her shoulder, sometimes pulling her close to kiss her, sometimes holding her at a distance. I saw an overstuffed album on the table, one he'd carefully prepared for her. Pages and pages of photographs of his past and of his children, and among them also a song that had been a kind of soulful anthem for him all his life— *"Mother, mother, if I've gone far, mother, you will know it. I'll build you royal palaces, my queen. . . . "*

"I shed tears of blood," the mother said in Arabic when she began setting out the story of her life, as Benda had asked. It was already late at night, and at a sign from one of the adults, the children were taken out of the room, as though they had begun to speak of things a child should not hear. "Tears of blood. They married me to your father at the age of fourteen," she told Benda. "To the Yemenite boy Moshe. You were born a year later. Your father played the oud and didn't work. I was alone and all he did was be jealous all the time and beat me. Everyone beat me—my father and your father." She told of evil times, when everyone's hand was raised against her. But when she said that everyone had beaten her, the entire room erupted in laughter, as if no one could imagine that the strong woman they knew as a mother and grandmother had once been weak and battered.

She divorced David's father and returned to her father's house. She didn't say explicitly where the boy David had been left. Did she take him with her, or had he remained, as people had told him, with his father, sleeping in his cradle while Moshe played the oud for wedding guests? In a neighborhood where Jews and Arabs lived next door to each other, one house touching another, she came to know a young Arab, the son of a storekeeper from Lydda who frequently came to Jaffa. In 1943, when David was five and his father was already serving in the British army overseas, she put him in an ultraorthodox orphanage, and her first son from her Arab husband was born. "I came every week to visit and took you home for the weekend," she told Benda.

"I don't remember you at all," Benda said tenderly, his words like a velvet-sheathed knife. He told the hushed room of the cruelty at the orphanage. His brothers and sisters listened to him talk about the loneliness and about his three years on the street. He didn't go into what he had told me about the thefts and the hunger, but his mother's face went stiff and she stopped smiling. At the age of seventy-three she was being brought before the family court for abandoning a child. The packed room became a tribunal. It was a hearing in which the defendant and the prosecutor sat in an embrace on a single couch. Without witnesses. Who was lying and who had forgotten, I asked myself. Had the mother visited him every weekend or had she simply disappeared from his life as if he'd never been? Was all trace of the boy erased from his mother's memory or was she lying to repair an old injustice that could no longer be righted?

Her profile was as sharp as a hatchet, her nose large, her chin jutting. "It was hard for me, too," she said. "I suffered a lot. I was alone for three years after leaving Mustafa. Here, both my arms were broken from the beatings." She displayed her damaged wrists. "My arms were broken in the orphanage, too," Benda said. "I'm not mad at you." He said it again, as if to himself.

A year after the birth of her first son to Mustafa her second son, the one who looked just like Benda, was born, and then she divorced Mustafa, their father. She drifted back and forth between the two peoples living adjacent to each other, and between her husbands, moving from here to there as if she did not recognize society's demands on a woman then, or did not notice the boundary that had already been drawn between the two nations. She was a wounded bird, wild, who broke all the rules, who crashed and rose again each time from the wreckage. And her children suffered a great deal from all of it. Life had been bad, she said. Mustafa had beaten her, like Moshe and like her father. After leaving Mustafa she returned to her parents' house on Zerach Brant Street, and her father received her without her Arab children. She lived there for three years, while her two sons from Mustafa grew up with their Palestinian grandparents. "When Mom came back from Tel

Aviv and came to take us," said the son who looked like Benda, "I didn't know who this woman was. I thought that Grandma was my mother." That brother had very soft eyes.

When Margalit returned to the family of her second husband, she married his brother, Fakri, by whom the rest of her children, boys and girls, were born. They lived in Lydda and witnessed the thunder that heralded the coming of the great war between the Jews and the Arabs. When the War of Independence broke out and Israeli forces arrived in Lydda, they fled to Nablus and Ramallah, and from there to Gaza, where they remained for a year.

In 1949 they crossed the border from Israel at night and reached Amman. The brother who looked like he could be Benda's twin told me that he vaguely remembered his grandfather leading him on a donkey in a convoy of refugees that crossed Israel at night. Twenty-two years after crossing Jordan as a girl in a convoy of Iraqi Jews on their way to Zion, Margalit now fled Zion for Jordan, borne on the donkeys of Palestinians. A refugee on both sides. Their wanderings ended in a camp at the bottom of one of the hills of Amman, where the eldest brother, the poorest of them all, lives to this day.

From that time, after the wanderings, they remember very well their grinding poverty as Palestinian refugees, in stifling tents in the camp. One of Margalit's sons told me how his mother had deftly mixed powdered milk she received from the UN with water and dried the resulting paste into *labaneh*, a sour Arab cheese, which her children sold to earn a few pennies. Adroitness and hard labor raised them, over the years, from the bottom of the hill where the refugee camp was to the spacious houses they live in today. Some of them went to college, and others worked morning to night to get out.

I found that they had Benda's hunger for success along with the Palestinian's longing for his home in the old country, about which they did not stop speaking, each one in his own way—some bitterly and others hopefully, some wistfully and some with resignation. The twin brother would the next day take Benda to a multi-roomed mansion he was erecting on a hill in Amman. A spacious stone sanctuary surrounded by a garden, looking out over the city and the refugee camps, over the mountains and the far horizon, where Israel's mountains were visible. And despite all his present success, the brother would in every conversation reiterate his right to return, if even only for a month, to the city of Lydda.

"Is the Allenby Cinema still there?" the elderly mother suddenly asked. "And the Carmel Market, and the Yemenite neighborhood?" Short sentences and the names of places on the city map returned to her as if after a long spell of amnesia; all at once everything that had been forbidden for years was permitted. In simple, basic, and unemotional language the mother spoke of her life—a story of suffering and wandering by a Jewish-Palestinian refugee, full of sorrow, beatings, and desertions. We left the mother's house after midnight, and sat a long while in the hotel lounge, because we could not sleep. Benda concealed a great torrent in his soul.

He was an orphan who'd suddenly discovered an event-filled family history, a tumultous past, and a present crowded with relatives. After years of silence and concealment, it looked as if a dam had broken, and might soon sweep away, in a massive flood, all the story's characters, if they did not take care.

At an hour between night and day we went up to our rooms, which had windows that looked out over the desert city. The air was warm and dry, and watchful soldiers sat at the entrance to the hotel. During the three days that followed, Benda traveled with his brothers in the city and its surroundings, getting as far as the red sandstone palaces of the chimerical kingdom of Petra. He went from his sister's house to his brother's flourishing business, surveying the construction of his identical brother's mansion, walking beside him as if they had never been separated. In the museum, inside the monument to the unknown Jordanian soldier, we saw the tattered gear of an Israeli pilot who had been shot down in the battle of Karameh. Benda began to shiver with cold, but each evening he made sure to go to the mother's house and sit with the family. When he bid her farewell she did not cry. Only on the telephone, when he called her house before crossing the bridge, did she break out sobbing, swearing that she would come visit Israel with her children. After the journey, in Tel Aviv, a good friend of Benda's told me that the whole story could easily have ended in quite another way. Given his resilient character, had the boy David gone with his mother to Jordan in the flight of 1949, had she taken him with her in her Palestinian wanderings, we might well have encountered him as a resolute enemy, or we might find him sitting opposite us, on the PLO side, during negotiations. It could have happened either way, and ending A is but a hairsbreadth away from ending B.

PETROV RUNS INTO
THE DESERT

ONE AUTUMN SATURDAY, at the time of the great wave of immigration from Russia, a mini-convoy of three vehicles was driving down the road near a kibbutz in the Negev, Israel's southern desert. All the passengers were new immigrants, friends who had left their Beersheba trailer camp to celebrate a birthday in a forest of several thousand trees planted in the middle of the wilderness. Vladislav Petrov's white Fiat Uno was the middle car. His cousin sat next to him and Petrov's wife, Ludmila, sat in the back. It's a narrow road that comes to a kind of double bend that, on the map, looks like half a noose. Petrov passed the car in front of him, then for some reason swerved to the left side of the road. Two of the wheels slid onto the soft shoulder. The car spun around in place and then rolled over five times before stopping, with its wheels in the air like the hooves of a dead beast.

The passengers scrambled out and were dumbfounded by the devastation the car had suffered. Ludmila saw that her husband's face was bloody with cuts from broken glass. He stood for a moment, his eyes wide open, without his glasses, and then he ran into the desert. She began to shout at him to stop but still doesn't know if he heard her. Petrov disappeared as if the earth had swallowed him up and since then she has had no husband.

When I arrived in Beersheba, two months had gone by since Petrov's run. I met with the Bedouin investigating officer, Azbarga, who knew the territory well, and had opened a thick file, stuffed with documents including the notices the police had put up as part of their search. The missing man's photograph showed him in a dark suit, with his glasses, a serious expression on his face, very different from the man who had emerged from under his upended car and run off as if his entire world had been destroyed. "I wait and wait," his wife Ludmila told me in their trailer. "What else can I do? Sometimes, at night, I cry."

Petrov's disappearance caught my attention because I thought that, in its own wretched way, it cast some light on the life of the Russian immigrants who had come to Israel to find a new home. One of Petrov's friends told me that everyone except the little children misses Russia. There they'd had homes, books, and friends, cities large and small, snow, joy, and sorrow. Petrov had met his wife in Leningrad when they were both in their thirties and both had children from previous marriages. He was thin, not tall, with gray eyes and a clipped, trim mustache; Ludmila was a good-looking, full-figured woman. While Petrov chauffeured passengers in his Leningrad taxi, she taught school. They had no children together and lived in comfort, spending time with friends, drinking, eating, and worried only about the ever-worsening situation in Russia. Letters arrived from Beersheba, where Ludmila's grandmother had settled, begging them to come. They didn't know if things really were so good in Beersheba or whether the grandmother was merely lonely and wanted company. But when the situation in Russia finally grew sufficiently grave, they immigrated straight to the desert city—together with a daughter, a granddaughter, and a capricious gray cat named Rezak.

Faulty immigrant reasoning, and a desire to save money, made them decide to live in Beersheba's huge neighborhood of ready-made caravan homes, one of dozens of such camps set up all over the country in the early 1990s to house the hundreds of thousands of newcomers from Russia. But whoever begins their life in Israel in a place of that sort seals their fate. The desert is a hard place in and of itself, and needs a lot of greenery to soften it for human habitation. The caravan neighborhood, where each home has just over two hundred square feet of floor space, is a merciless patch of desolation. The houses are made of cheap, graceless material and stand on bare earth that sends up a cloud of dust with each footstep. Electrical wires stretch overhead, thin bars separating human from sky. Everything is sad and hopeless, and in the winter it is very cold. Ludmila found cleaning work, and Petrov worked a bit in construction. At night they dreamed of Leningrad. Not about the fleshpots, but about their apartment in the big city, where they had friends. Here they were refugees. From the window they saw desert. Petrov, the former cab driver, began dreaming about steering wheels. He missed his car. Maybe he was longing for a property of his own—a new car, fragrant with new upholstery and gasoline, that could take him from the trailer camp to someplace else. He bought a brand-new white Fiat the summer before the accident. The money came from a bank loan.

The Fiat stood next to the caravan house. A cute Italian car with an engine that made a nice hum. But no money was left over for insurance and Ludmila was worried—even though Petrov said that he was an excellent driver and that there was nothing to be concerned about. When I began to look for him, I went, under Ludmila's direction, to a huge building site in the Negev, where new immigrants build homes for newer immigrants. Two of Petrov's friends and I crouched in an unfinished stairwell. They told me that Petrov was a good guy, but he was always anxious and felt lost. "There was something in his face that moved all the time," one of them told me. "He didn't feel at home here. If he thought about going back, he didn't talk about it, because he had nothing left there, no apartment, no family." During the week he would work and sleep in the unfinished building. Every night before going to sleep he drank a single shot glass of vodka, no more, no less—not to get drunk, only to help him forget the life that sometimes seemed so shitty that he'd tell his friend, "I've got this urge to put an end to it." He'd go home only on weekends, driving his car with great caution in order to protect it. When it flipped over he may have felt that all was lost. Without insurance, injured, in shock, he'd reached the end of the road. What little comfort he'd had, had gone.

I went with Petrov's friends to the site of the accident, near the kibbutz. A cracked front windshield still lay on the roadside, with a license sticker in one corner. One man at the kibbutz remembered the incident well because he drove the kibbutz ambulance to the scene of the accident when the emergency call came in. When he arrived, the overturned vehicle reeked strongly of vodka, and the people were pointing in horror at the hills and wilderness into which Petrov had disappeared. From the point where the windshield lay, the hill rolled down into a kind of depression and then rose up again. The desert landscape was rutted and blasted; the first rain had yet to fall. It was all hills and wadis, chalk hills and huge spaces empty of man.

On the day of his disappearance the police sent forces into the field. The searchers found, along the most likely path of his flight, a small Bedouin shepherd girl who related that she had been sitting with her herd on a little green hillock when a blood-soaked and frightened man had come along. He had spoken unclearly and asked for water. She gave him water from a plastic container and warmed up a little tea for him. He had sat there for a quarter of an hour and then went off. When he descended from the hill he continued over fields and more hills until she could no longer see him. The police investigators hoped, as they always do, that carrion birds would show them where the body was, or that maybe he would return safely to his caravan home. But neither of those things happened. Ludmila, in despair, went to two fortune-tellers. One of them saw Petrov dead, while the other said that he was alive, in the dunes, living with the Bedouin. The police suspected that he might have headed for an Arab village. A hostile village stood on one of the pale hills on the other side, within walking distance. The open spaces of the desert were no longer safe. "Maybe he's hiding under a false identity," a police officer said to me. "Maybe he walked down the railroad ties or on the asphalt and we lost his tracks." But Petrov was half-blind without his glasses, and he had no money to begin a new life in another place. No money, no inner strength, and no hope. I walked from the road to see the security officer of the kibbutz on whose lands Petrov had disappeared. He's always driving around in his jeep, with a rifle and a radio, keeping his eyes open. He said that the whole place was full of old wells and caves where a person could rot without anyone knowing. There are tunnels from the time of the Bar-Kochba rebellion, the ruins of Arab villages, and the remains of Bronze Age settlements. While we were sitting in the dining hall he had the idea that I might want to go out into the field on a Polaris dune buggy and have a look around. The kibbutz made some extra money offering dune-buggy trips to tourists and had a well-kept garage with an impressive fleet of small, sinewy vehicles, easy to drive, with thick tires that eat up the hard ground with wild glee. If a few of those had gone out searching for Petrov immediately after the accident, they would have found him.

We set out in a cloud of dust to the place of the broken glass, and from there we sailed down the hill to the little shepherd girl's hillock. The fields undulated into Wadi Shikma, where, in a dampness that survived even in the summer, a green, tangled line of bushes grew. Bedouin apparently stop by there; we found an old car battery, a girl's copper bracelet, and, close by, an abandoned Arab village made up entirely of deep caves with large yards still marked out and family wells. Everywhere there were the signs of shepherds and hikers who had come by—the feathers of a pigeon that had been eaten, empty turtle shells, and spent hunters' cartridges. For hours we moved across the land split by the wadi but found no sign of the vanished immigrant Petrov.

I returned, all dusty, to Ludmila, who no longer believed that her beloved Petrov would ever return. His broken glasses rested like eyes on the caravan's table. The sight of her husband running into the desert was like a scar in her memory. What had he seen there with his short-sighted eyes? Had the bright desert made him homesick for the snows of Leningrad? Had he suddenly noticed something familiar and run to it? Ludmila asked herself those questions day and night, and they tormented her like an interrogation that had no end.

A year after I'd been there the Bedouin investigator from Beersheba contacted me. He'd called to tell me that a guy who'd gone walking in the desert to search for migrating birds had found Petrov hanging from a tree in one of the wadis. His body was desiccated from months in the sun, and his eyes had been picked out. Ludmila was no longer in her caravan. She had moved with her daughter, granddaughter, and the gray cat Rezak to some other place, and no one could give me her new address.

TWO HEROES

I WENT TO THE Tirat Ha-Carmel Psychiatric Hospital
to see a patient who, after twenty years of electric shocks,
got himself out and returned to life. He lives in a small
apartment outside the hospital, and now comes within
its walls only to help others escape terror. I'd visited a
number of psychiatric institutions while following up
on some Israeli soldiers who had returned thirty years
ago after a decade as POWs in Syria. They'd been hospitalized for the rest of their lives. My whole life I'd
interviewed Israelis on the free side, and I thought that
I knew every corner of the country. But here I found an
entire world hidden behind the madhouse fence, a tiny
universe containing thousands who had not withstood
the tribulations of the Israeli way of life. A seething,
agonized world with a sound like a screech in a sealed

room. Even during election campaigns, when every vote counts and politicians find their way into every forgotten corner, none of them hug mental patients to win their support. The mentally ill are farther away from people's hearts than the dead.

Israel is a land of immigrants; relatively few of the country's older inhabitants were born here. Most people's parents or grandparents came from other homelands and endured displacement or Holocaust, deportation or other trials. There are children who fled the Nazis, war refugees, survivors of horror treks through Ethiopia, people who stole across the border from Syria and escaped empty-handed from the Caucasus. Many reached their heart's desire, sweated, and established families—but there were also those who fell by the wayside, mute witnesses more eloquent than any historian to what happened along the way. "When you enter the private world of the great majority of my patients, you go through the gates of Israeli history," the doctor said. "You discover, from their stories, how the country was founded and how heavy a price was paid in the separation of families, homelessness, and agony. You find out what this country is made of."

At the hospital I heard about Shraga, the man from the Holocaust who pulled himself out of his illness, and also about an Ethiopian boy who had lost his mind in a caravan camp when he suddenly remembered everything that had happened to him along the way. He'd begun to see ghosts everywhere. The boy refused to talk to me, but Shraga willingly agreed. He's an older man, and it's all already settled at the bottom of his soul and found its resting place there. Even the specters that persecuted him are worn out.

When I arrived, he was waiting for me in the psychiatrist's office. The three of us sat in the cool room on a searing summer day, and there Shraga told me the story of his life. Afterwards I spoke briefly with the physician, Dr. Danny Enoch, and it turned out that we had fought in the same place in the 1973 war, and that this doctor who sat quietly to one side throughout my interview with Shraga had received a medal for his heroism in a Syrian minefield.

So it turned out that I'd come to talk to the patient but found the doctor as well. I listened to both stories—that of the patient who'd collapsed into mental illness and returned to life, and that of the doctor who'd almost lost his life in a minefield and only thereafter understood how close he himself had been to shell shock and collapse. As I listened I became ever more aware that here were two heroes—not just the army doctor who'd won glory, but also Shraga, the patient, who as a boy had been a partisan fighter in a Ukrainian forest. Those deeds erupted years later like a volcano and brought on a twenty-year hospitalization with electric shocks and insulin therapy. An official state hero and an anonymous hero, unrecognized—like all of those who had excelled "there."

Both doctor and patient had experienced what Dr. Enoch himself called "halted time." "It doesn't matter if you talk about it immediately afterwards or fifty years later—it doesn't matter when you talk to the person who experienced it—there is that unit of time of the traumatic event which he'll always describe to you as if it were happening this instant. It's alive and full of mental energy," said Dr. Enoch. "And according to my theory, so long as no dialogue is created between the halted time and progressive time, the person is wounded and should be classified as posttraumatic." Dr. Enoch and Shraga, the doctor and the former patient, have both learned to live at peace with their halted time. That similarity between these two Israeli heroes existed only in my imagination, as I listened to both of them in the same room. When they were photographed they did not touch each other. They preserved a distance between the man who had been a patient who returned from madness, and the other man, a well-known psychiatrist, a decorated officer, and the director of the hospital where the conversation took place.

Shraga is a man of average height who is missing the tip of one finger. A baseball cap shades his face, which is tanned like that of a tractor driver. He has an excellent memory for the details of the harsh things he endured "there." When he speaks of his lost father or mother, he repeats several sentences over and over, such as the description of his tall, beautiful mother, and the departure of his father, and the fact that perhaps he is alive somewhere in the world, far from his children, but has not made contact with them. Shraga was born in the Polish city of Lvov, where his father had a wagon with two horses. His mother sold, here and there, saccharin and other materials that were in demand. They lived a tranquil life with his sisters, one older, one younger than Shraga. There was a house, a family, a school where he went to first grade, a few small friends his age. But when Shraga was seven years old, everything was destroyed in a single moment. The Germans came to his house and the familiar world around him disappeared in an instant.

His father fled with his wagon to Russia and did not have time to come to take them. Holding her year-old baby in her arms, their mother told Shraga and his twelve-year-old sister: "Run away to wherever you can, just don't stay here, save yourselves." Shraga remembers the kiss his mother gave him—and that was it. "What can a seven-year-old boy do?" They had nothing with them at all. He doesn't remember a bundle with food or anything else, everything took place in a great rush, in panic. The first night the two children slept in the street and two days later they were in the forest. In a second he'd been plucked from his life, from his family, from his home and friends, from everything that surrounds the little life of a boy, from everything that is meant to protect him and prepare him for life, and to guard his soul against the terror and troubles around him.

Overnight they became a twelve-year-old girl and a seven-year-old boy who lived off fruit and water they found in the forest. "The forest was full of good things and we didn't lack food." To this day he remembers the forest as a divine cornucopia and has no memory of either hunger or fear. At night they slept and listened to the animals around them, and when they reached the first village, his sister told him that his name from now on was Misha Cherkewitz, the name of their non-Jewish neighbor, so that no one would know he was a Jew. And he shouldn't let anyone see his wee-wee. So his name and identity were also lost, and so was his sister—she went to a different village because she was afraid they would discover his circumcision and kill her as well.

Shraga became a shepherd for a gentile who took him in as a non-Jewish orphan. The life of an abandoned boy with poor, hard-hearted farmers has already been described by Jerzy Kosinski in his disturbing novel *The Painted Bird*. It was not a place of compassion, and Shraga told me that later, when he was a fighter in the forest and had a Schmeisser submachine gun, he considered going back to kill that gentile—the gentile who made him responsible for the small flock, beat him sometimes, yet accepted him into his family.

How does a seven-year-old boy understand what he needs to hide in order to live?

"A boy in trouble understands everything."

For two years he lived with the sheep and didn't lack food. As he told me about his life there, he stuck to the facts, and I had to ask him repeatedly about his feelings before he said that at night he had cried sometimes, "and I missed my family horribly, as if there were huge stones pounding in my heart. You feel that you have no mother. There's no one in the world looking out for you." When Shraga took a break for lunch, Dr. Enoch explained to me that people like Shraga have accomplished massive repression and that they are naturally shielded from the events that aroused anxiety so severe that it led to breakdown. "They always tell only the facts, but anyone who listens, like you, for example, fills in the picture with his own fantasies. You, with your free imagination and thought, fill in the spaces between the facts." That's what this story is: fact, empty space, and fantasy.

During the lunch break I went outside for a while, to the garden in front of the hospital. It's a relatively new building, full of light, and the lobby is lined with the paintings of Segal, one of the patients. There, at the entrance, I heard the heartrending sobs of a small boy who seemed that very moment to have been yanked out of Shraga's story. The hospital guard, equipped with a pistol, circled the child helplessly. "Why is he crying?" I asked the guard. He pointed to a large sign stating that the entry of children was forbidden, alongside the prohibitions against bringing in firearms, pocketknives, and various glass items. His father had gone in and left him outside for a moment. The little boy was crying "Daddy, Daddy . . ." and tried again and again to go inside, and each time he was blocked by the guard. I bought him a can of strawberry soda and he trembled and fell silent. Afterwards he attached himself to the can as if it were a breast. He discovered its sweetness and stopped crying, then sat on the fence, gripping the can, and waited for his father. I thought of Shraga's first night in the forest, of how close he must have stuck to his sister, and then of her disappearance, of how he slept in the gentile's house, and of his time alone with the sheep, dispossessed of his name and parents and identity.

Without a photograph or document or an object of any sort to grasp or remember by, the sweet past was left like a bomb in the memory of the boy Shraga. Two identities existed simultaneously within him: the real one, laden with longing; and the false one, meant to protect him. "And there are things," Dr. Enoch told me, "that are impossible to take from a person, things that belong just to him. He'll never be able to make others a part of them—and that's true about Shraga, and about me, and perhaps you as well. We've been through horrifying war experiences, each in his own way, and we have no way of sharing them with people close to us. That creates a great sense of loneliness. There's an inner scream that goes unheard, and it is like the silence of the lambs."

Once, after almost two years with the gentile owner of the herd, Shraga went to see his sister in the next village over. When he found her, she told him, "Go back to your village. Don't try to play any tricks. Mom and the baby are dead. The Germans murdered them."

"And I said to myself, if that's so, I'll go and avenge them. By that point I only had the farmer's clothes and I didn't remember a lot from before. I couldn't remember her name or much else, but a good picture of Mother remained in my memory, tall and pretty, and I heard the farmers talking about the partisans in the forests around us, that they always needed children to help blow up trains. One day when I was herding the sheep— it was the middle of the day—I stole a horse from the family. I already knew how to ride well, and I ran away to the forest, fifteen miles from Kiev." He rode for several days and didn't see a single person in the forest, as the war was advancing and people had run away or hidden. "One morning a man with a rifle stood facing me." Shraga asked him where children could enlist, then freed the horse and followed the man to the commander. They put him together with twenty-three other children. They all lived and slept in an underground bunker, partisan kids, orphans who had come from all sorts of places. "And no one knew I was a Jew. When I pissed or washed, I was always alone, and even when we bathed in the river, I kept my underpants on so they wouldn't see I was circumcised, because they were Ukrainians and I thought they'd kill me." The children were taught how to read and write, and to handle mines with long fuses. "And I knew that I wanted to avenge my mother's death.

"One night they took twenty kids and gave us twenty-five pounds of explosives and fuse and everything else we needed and showed us the way. We were all nine to twelve years old, and we went and put it under the train track, and we lit a ten-yard-long fuse and we waited until the train came and saw it go up in the air and fall apart and people were screaming inside, and we laughed out of joy and ran back to the camp. I had a Schmeisser submachine gun that was more precious to me than anything else in the world, and we'd use it to kill a sheep or a cow and then we'd drag it back to the camp to eat. We all slept—twenty-four kids—on boards underground, and we huddled together to keep warm under blankets we took from the Germans, and we talked at night about our parents and what had happened to them. 'Our children,' was what the partisan women who came to our room like mothers called us.

"I was already an eleven-year-old man, strong and well-developed, and I had learned to fight for what was mine. And when the war ended I jumped on a truck, but I was small and didn't manage to climb up all the way and rode three hundred miles on the running board. In Lvov I found that our house had been destroyed." Only his sister remained alive. Shraga, who had reassumed his Jewish name, which was all that was left to him from the past, with the exception of his sister, went to one of the transit camps in Germany where the Zionist movement was organizing groups of young people for settlement in Palestine. In 1948 he went to Israel, to Kibbutz Nitzanim. During his many years in the hospital, his friend from the kibbutz, David, would come visit him— but Shraga did not know his last name.

In 1951, at the age of seventeen, Shraga enlisted in the army, in the combat engineer corps. No one there knew anything about the boy's past, or how, years before, he had been a brave little partisan who'd blown up trains. The past had been erased, no one there took an interest in him, or loved him for his courage. Everything remained "there." He became a tractor and heavy equipment operator and paved the roads of the country that had just now come into existence—from Mitzpeh Ramon to Tel Mutila and Dardara. His sister married and had a family, and he went to live with them from time to time, working as a tractor driver for the Solel Boneh construction company. He was a solitary young man, with difficult memories, who began to have horrible headaches. They came more and more frequently until one day, during a stint of reserve duty in the Galilee, he felt that his head was actually exploding between his shoulders.

He was taken to the hospital, and there he remained for twenty years. The doctors in Acre classified him as schizophrenic, that catch-all diagnosis that once encompassed everyone who had lost his mind or who had suffered a psychotic crisis or who got left by the side of the road. And so in 1961, twenty years after his mother had hastily sent him off to fend for himself, his lost childhood exploded in his head, and he had no one to protect him. His sister threw up her hands in despair. "I received electric shocks and injections, and sometimes I thought to myself that I had no parents to look after me, and I wondered why after I had been such a healthy, strong kid during the war, and I'd survived the Nazis and everything else, that here, of all places, it should fall on me. All the memories broke through inside me like a volcano that had been stopped up for a long time."

He was transferred from one institution to another, along with his medical file, which showed no change in his diagnosis. "Sometimes I missed the partisan days, and I thought that I ought to get up and fight for my life like I had back there, because when you fall, everyone tramples you. I felt a terrible longing in those years to see human beings, not sick people." It was only thirteen years ago that he rose from the ashes. He had ended up in the Tirat Ha-Carmel institution, living in the chronic-illness ward, a place for patients they had given up on. It was an open ward, and he was allowed to work in the carpentry shop. Someone finally took notice of him—a doctor and a social worker named Moria, and then some others—and he underwent rehabilitation and moved into a little apartment in the town of Tirat Ha-Carmel, in time becoming a deputy counselor for other patients. "But the lost time, the twenty years will never come back, I know." Every morning at six he leaves his apartment in order to sit with the guys in the rehab unit, to turn on the water heater for them, drink coffee, and talk about life. He's connected to the world outside through his sister and her children and grandchildren, and via the television in his apartment. He watches German television channels, especially likes soccer, and news a bit as well. "And that's my life," he told me. According to Dr. Enoch, "Shraga is a success story, maybe limited, but whole. He found his place and he has no more claims against the world and his creator. In this respect he lives a life that is perhaps small in your eyes, but it is intrinsically whole."

I saw a tiny painting on the wall above Enoch's desk, so tiny, like a sticker on a child's schoolbook, that I had to get very close to make out that it was a picture of a tree growing out of the middle of a table. His office also had an old vacuum-tube radio and a chess set—that being the primary hobby of the introverted doctor. He is fifty years old, born exactly ten years after Shraga, but in Israel, so he has no memories from "there." When he was four years old the War of Independence broke out and he was kept in a bomb shelter, and during the 1967 war he was studying medicine in France, after following the usual Israeli path of high school and army. After he returned, his studies completed, the Yom Kippur War broke out, and Enoch became the doctor of an infantry battalion. He was with the unit through its bad days in the war—the loss of the Mount Hermon outpost and the attempts to retake it that cost so many lives. But the time etched in Enoch's memory as the great trauma of his life was the year that followed the war, during the war of attrition in the territory that had been conquered from the Syrians at the end of the hostilities. It was a rocky piece of basaltic land that was constantly peppered with well-aimed enemy fire. "I treated about two hundred and fifty wounded men from the brigade there," and there the thing happened that got him a medal but which is imprinted in his memory as halted time—and which nearly afflicted him with paralyzing shell shock.

His battalion manned several outposts on the basalt terrain. Twice a week Enoch went out on violent patrols with the battalion, during which every soldier was in Syrian sights and vulnerable. One night Enoch was assigned to a patrol of this type and sent out to harass the enemy. He set out with twenty soldiers and officers to penetrate Syrian territory and pick off a few Syrian soldiers in their outposts. It was a mild moonlit night and the detachment moved in two columns, every boulder casting a shadow like that of an enemy fighter.

The captain, who was first in line, stepped on an antipersonnel mine and lost a foot, and two medics who rushed to him also lost feet, as did seven other soldiers who were caught in that unmarked minefield, eighteen miles inside Syrian territory. Enoch, being the doctor and the only officer who was still in one piece, moved among the wounded with morphine and IVs, probing for land mines with his rifle barrel before every step he took. Between bandaging the remains of his men's feet, he was in radio contact with the battalion commander to arrange for a rescue party to meet them at a rendezvous point and take them back. The ten sound soldiers each carried a wounded man on his back and returned to Israeli territory through seven nightmare hours under Syrian fire. "During the event you don't think about anything except the action, but sometime later I took in what had happened and how I had in fact done something suicidal." Enoch returned whole and was decorated. Then he found himself going out on more and more missions in order to suit a heroic image that was not his. For years he also had that same sensation of "halted time," the hours in the minefield and on the way back, "and the process of understanding deeply what had happened to me took a long time."

When I ask him whether his battle experience allows him to give better care to people like Shraga who have had difficult experiences, he hesitates. Afterwards he answers in a roundabout way that avoids any expression of emotion. What's more, in all the time that I sat with the sick man and his doctor—several hours—and when we had our pictures taken together in the garden, absolutely no physical contact transpired between them. They each still belonged to two different wars—two wars of the Jews that might as well have taken place on two different planets.

THE MAN WHO FELL
INTO A PUDDLE

ONLY AT THE END OF HIS MOTHER'S LIFE, when Yechiel Segal was himself already close to retirement and she was lying in an old-age home that was rapidly eating up what remained of her money, did they get somewhat closer. Each day after work he would get on the bus at Rehovot's central bus station and get off in Herzliyya. Then he'd walk the three miles to the old-age home, where he would take her out to the garden in her wheelchair and listen to her torrent of anger at the world. At the old-age home, diapered old men and women whose arms no longer moved rested in their beds, and the nurses set the tables before every meal—fork, soup spoon, teaspoon, and napkin next to each plate. Then they shoveled everything into the old people's mouths. His mother was paralyzed but her mind was as clear as that of a young girl, and she would always tell Yechiel: "I'm mad at God for not taking me." But what he was waiting for her to say to him was: "Zuza, do you love me?" Or: "Zuza, I loved you." A man, even when he's eighty years old, waits for his mother to tell him she loves him, and God help the boy whose mother doesn't love him. But that's how it was for him when he was a boy. She had no patience and no time for him. So every day during her final year, when she lay there, he traveled that whole way and waited, maybe today she'll say it. But she was sunk so deep in the bitterness of an old woman whose whole life had been beautiful and now here she was lying in her own filth, that for him to wait for her to say that single word of love was like expecting a man without legs to skip rope. "I needed it like I needed air to breathe, the one good word, and go try to understand how that little thing turned into something of the highest importance for me—and Mother died without saying it."

Segal described that entire desperate wait, if that is how it could be described, as we sat together on a bench in a small park in Rehovot, near a nursery school. There was a playground there—a slide and a sandbox—and an old building that housed the city's first well. Segal rested a flat carton on his lap and sketched the park and the pump-house wall on a piece of paper that had once been used for another drawing. That's how he sat every day, alone, facing the old building and drawing. Gray locks of hair fell over his forehead and his boyish blue eyes, which suddenly looked to me like the two colorful wings of his long, sharp nose. The act of talking with him—and this happens sometimes with poets or artists, whose words contain a magic that makes everything around them soar—made me see things in the particular light that he cast on them. His tale of his mother reminded me of sentences I'd heard from a poet some time before. Like a late, strangled call directed at all mothers: Please, really love your children, because if you don't you doom them to despair and loss and a life of great confusion and to a search that never ends. Only the fortunate among the unloved will be so astute as to translate their pain into poems or sweeten their lives with paintings.

I heard about Segal from the poet Natan Zach, who loved this hidden artist and thought more highly of him than he did of other painters who get thousands of dollars for each picture. Zach made his acquaintance years ago, when both of them were members of a restless young crowd that in the 1950s migrated between cheap cafés in Tel Aviv and Haifa, or at first sat uneasily, half off their chairs, on the fringes of Kasit, the Tel Aviv literary hangout, sharing among them a single cup of tea. Most of them were uprooted new immigrants. There was Marian Merinal, who hanged herself from an electric pole, and Pinchas Burnstein, who killed himself in New York; Tzvika Milstein, who had artistic success in Paris, and Arieh Ekstein, who wandered as far as desolate Rosh Pina. There was Braunstein, who lost his mind—and several others. They looked as if they'd been predestined for devastation, because of their talent, or their loneliness. Few of them survived.

The Man Who Fell into a Puddle

Zach brought Yechiel with him to the Frak Café so I could meet him. This Dizengoff Street coffeehouse has an astoundingly hideous decor and the air of a place whose finest days passed years ago. When I arrived, Zach and the ascetic-looking Segal were already sitting there, along with Segal's radiant-faced wife, Rivka, and another older man called Doctor, Segal's good friend. Zach sent us to a side table so we could converse quietly. Segal sat facing me, slightly bent, and immediately began speaking in his customary candid, awkward way, angling the whole time for some evasive truth. He sprayed words as an ax sprays splinters.

When the two of them—he and his twin sister, Meira—were five years old, they immigrated to Israel from Kishinev in Russia. His father, Matityahu, was already a well-known political activist who attended all the Zionist congresses. His mother was an educated woman of acclaimed beauty over whom Russian officers dueled and around whom other men buzzed like bees. They made their domicile in the heart of Tel Aviv, in a prosperous neighborhood appropriate to their sense of the class of people they belonged to. The parents were preoccupied all day with their business and love affairs, and during those moments when they found themselves in the same place, they fought and screamed and generally poisoned the atmosphere around them. "And my sister Meira and I were left to our own devices. We never left each other—not on the beach or in the neighborhood, on the street, and certainly not at night in a home that was devoid of our parents, who had gone out to a party and wouldn't return before dawn. I was an ugly and gloomy kid who looked nothing like my attractive father or mother or sister, and I had a strange sort of lump here, on my chest, a kind of deformation of the ribs, which were crushed during birth, and I was self-conscious about that throughout my whole childhood. I bore it like a cross."

At the age of thirteen he was struck by meningitis and for months flitted between life and death. From that time on, he did not go to school. And even though he came from a family of means, he took nothing from home and started off as a manual laborer, which is what he would remain his entire life. He worked on a loom in a Jerusalem factory, and afterwards as a messenger boy on a bicycle—his lifelong vehicle. At the same time, he was desperately in love with a girl named Etka, the daughter of a well-known actor, who was beautiful and surrounded by a thousand boys. "I loved her with a deadly love, and I was always seeking love." As he pronounced the word "love," over and over again, through his teeth, it sounded like the last exhalation of a drowning man, choked and searing.

At the age of sixteen, Yechiel Segal's life turned upside down. Yechiel, whose sister called him Zuza, while others seldom called him at all, and from whose chest a little lump stuck out, enlisted in the British army. That was in 1942, and an ordnance company took him on as a lugger of shells and a filler of mines. "Those were the finest years of my life—five years in which our people went through hell, but for me it was good.

Life is, after all, depression and happiness, built out of tiny things, *pitzkalach*. The English treated me well, I had friends there and I traveled to Lebanon and Cyprus, Egypt and the western desert, Italy, you name it. I lugged shells and I was indispensable. I worked like a dog and I was happy."

During that time he didn't stop drawing even for a moment. "And there was a moment of happiness that came my way in the army, and it gave meaning to my entire life. My company was on the move as part of a rotation of battalions in Italy, in the winter, riding in simple freight cars. The train stopped for a while and the officers told us to get off the train, to stretch our legs a little. It was dark and I jumped straight into an icy puddle of water, and when I landed in it I didn't want to get up again. I didn't mind it. I felt free, I turned into sand, into stars, into stones, water, fish. I didn't know any more who, what, or why, but this transcendent sense of happiness came over me, and the memory of it has pursued me ever since—my whole life I've been seeking to return to the serenity of that puddle, and I just can't find it. It gave meaning to my life, if a living creature is capable of attaining a moment like that, of being at one with the universe, with God. Even in drunkenness and insanity the memory of that moment would not leave me, and fifty electric shocks couldn't pry it out of my head."

When he was discharged from the army he returned to his parents' home in Tel Aviv, with 140 English pounds in demobilization pay in his pocket. The city was full of discharged soldiers looking for work, and Segal wandered around until he found a job in a factory that made kettles and other metal household utensils. During the ten years in which the country was founded, war broke out, and in which he married Rivka Levkowitz, he made kettles by day and in the evenings hung out with his bohemian crowd—Milstein and Zach, and Marian the artist, and sometimes Avidan. Endless walks and sitting in the Milo Club and talking till morning. Throughout that time his friend Tzvika Milstein kept hold of him. Milstein stays closely in touch with Segal to this day from Paris, and it was Milstein who pushed him to study painting. Segal, who was always broke, sketched in charcoal and hauled some tubes and turpentine here and there so he could paint. At the end of every day at the kettle factory, he ran to wash his hands, grab a sandwich, and go to paint. The painter Avni knew and loved him, and others also quickly became acquainted with the talent of this man without time and money who drew by the grace of God, a natural-born artist.

But at the end of the 1950s, when the kettle factory went bust and no other livelihood was to be found, his Tel Aviv days were over, and Segal's friends lost track of him for many years. They heard only that he had gone to the Negev and that he was drinking. But it wasn't that simple. He had heard that in the Negev there were free apartments and work, so with his partner, Rivka, he packed up what few belongings he had and went south to look for employment. For his entire life, painting would be a hobby alongside hard work and crushing poverty, a kind of punishment he imposed on himself. In the desert his son and daughter were born. Held fast by the cables of his poverty, Segal ran from one job to another. They lived in a small town of ugly public housing developments, on land so parched by the acrid heat that trees would not grow. During the days he cleaned the little police station and at night the lit-up café on the road, and sold cigarettes to truck drivers who stopped for a break. He didn't have a moment to touch his painting.

"We were as lonely as dogs there. When my son was a year old, Rivka and I prepared a little celebration from stuff a truck had brought from Beersheba. We bought and prepared and we invited people who worked with me there to the birthday party. We stood at the door and waited and not a soul came. The loneliness there was like on the moon, and it stayed with me like a wound, that baby's birthday party." Once when Segal rode up to Tel Aviv for a day to visit his parents, he heard on the bus that his father had died. The news caught him on the road, and when he arrived in the city they asked him to identify the body. "I saw the body of an utterly broken man. My father was retired, at the age I am today, and without a career or friends, he sat alone on Dizengoff Street or dozed off in the movies. This man who'd spent his entire life partying and being loved, who had always been surrounded by friends—he was so depressed he went up to the roof of a building and jumped." So the father departed and what remained was a connection of a sort with the mother. From about that time he no longer saw his twin sister.

After about four years in the Negev the work dried up there also, and the Segals were forced to go north, moving into a dilapidated shack they rented in an orange grove in Rehovot, surrounded by little kitchen gardens belonging to farmers of Romanian extraction. For half a year Segal made a living by killing laboratory rats that had been infected in experiments at the Weizmann Institute of Science. He demonstrated for me how he did it—two fingers fixed firmly around the rodent's neck and with the other hand a pull of the tail, and the neck is broken. "I came home each day with scratches on my hands, because they would scratch me, trying to escape. It was incredibly horrifying work with Professor Katzir, deep depression, because I don't even step on cockroaches, and here I was murdering thousands of rats and mice with my own hands."

Half a year later a miracle happened when Segal found the job he would work at happily for twenty-five years. He became a water-meter reader for the Rehovot municipality. "I'd ride my bike through the orange groves and farms, happy and my own master. Me, my bicycle, my pad and pencil—and, from that time, a bottle as well, because I'd begun to turn into something of a drunk. I made real progress at drinking. I'm a horrible coward, I have anxieties and fears and I'm afraid of my own shadow, but when I drank I dulled the fears, and I enjoyed it so much that I became the village lush. With a flask in my pocket, I rode a little, took a gulp, read a meter, and I didn't make a single mistake in twenty-five years." He'd work diligently to read two hundred meters in one day so that he could spend the next five days drinking. "People would come and say that drunk is making mistakes, but I always proved I was right, because the drink only made me more focused. I didn't bother anyone and I wasn't a disgusting drunk—at worst sad sometimes. We lived in a ruin in an orange grove owned by a vicious landlord—my wife and I, two children, a donkey, a horse, and a dog. I devoted myself to the children and I'd cook for them when they came home from school, and make dinner for my wife, Rivka, and build kites and bows and arrows, and in the evening I'd take a bottle and sit under a tree by the house and watch the sunset and the fields and feel happy." As for painting . . . he didn't paint anymore.

One day Rivka heard about a treatment center for alcoholics. And even though Segal thought that he was fine with the bottle and wasn't doing any harm to anyone, he agreed to go there because he was afraid that his employers' patience might eventually run out and they'd fire him. He got a month's leave from the city, and at the treatment center he swore he would never drink again. They sent him from there to a painting class for adults, because they heard from him that he'd once liked to paint and they wanted him to find some sort of pursuit that would help him stay cured. "I hadn't painted for years, except when I'd go to an Arab village to read a meter and I'd draw a horse or donkey for the kids there." But when he went back to painting in the class, he began going there every day and painting with a mania that grew more and more intense, "and I held on to painting like it was the horns of the altar, and I'm addicted to it to this day."

His friend Milstein came for a visit from Paris and found him like a broken vessel in his devastation, in his miserable dilapidated house. He gave him paints and materials, and together with Zach they arranged for his first exhibition. Other shows followed. The visitors were moved by the paintings of the man who had hidden for so many years and who had not belonged to any circle of artists, and of whose works no collection existed because he had destroyed almost all of them. He would paint on the back of a poster he tore off an announcement board, or on the back of an earlier painting he'd done. He was always seeking out whatever cheap paper was at hand, and afterwards he'd crumple it up and throw it in the trash. "Because when you collect paper you choke, so I threw them away, I didn't hoard anything, and each day meant the promise of a new painting." He would remain, as was his habit, in the shadows, not selling but sometimes giving them away or discarding them.

Segal did indeed keep himself from fame with the same force that he had pursued love. Nothing changed in his life until he retired. He rode, painted, didn't drink, raised his children, cooked, and looked, and his world ended only when his job ended and he went out on pension. Without bicycle trips to water meters, without his travels through the orange groves, he suddenly sank.

He'd go for walks each day with his wife and his baby grandson, whom they watched for their daughter, and he felt a horrible emptiness. Suddenly he stopped talking, regressed. "I didn't speak to anyone and I didn't draw a line. I lay on my bed under the blanket and got up only to drive my wife to despair." For two years he was overwhelmed by a paralyzing depression and barely moved. He suffered profoundly and descended deep into the abyss, until one of the doctors who knew about his artwork suggested that he go with his wife to the city's older streets, the ones he'd once loved, and come back and describe for her—the doctor—what he'd seen.

To accommodate his wife and the doctor, as he'd wanted to accommodate people all his life, he went to the south side of the city with Rivka and a small child's sketch pad and a pencil and looked for a turquoise window and a spiral banister. "But I wasn't able to draw a straight line. My hands trembled. And I told myself: If you can't draw a straight line, you die on the spot. All around me shouting, noise, people asking themselves what that bent and crazy old man was doing—and all I was trying to do was draw a straight line. I filled an entire pad with the old houses on a street in the southern part of the city. The paralyzed body broke free, the hands trembled less. That straight line held me and pulled me out of the morass. They made me an exhibit. A miracle happened to me. Whoever dreamed that I'd go out for coffee again with my wife and with Natan and the guys, that I'd have a show."

At the time I interviewed him, Segal was already

entirely caught up in painting. Each night he got up at one and painted till morning. Things from the newspaper, or a water pitcher, anything he saw. Once a week he stood with his friend Doctor in front of a painting at the museum and studied every detail. On other days he took a small child's chair, a piece of cardboard, watercolors, a cup full of water and a brush, put everything in a shopping basket, and walked until he found an old house, and then sat down to draw. Always old houses, and sometimes a little boy in the undergrowth, if one passed by the old painter—everything out of wistfulness for that time when he himself was a little boy, playing with his twin sister on Ha-Maggid Street, while dusk fell over the city and no one called him to come home.

THE SIN OF
THE BEDOUIN BOY

IF THERE IS A HELL, then it's there, in that white-hot place where the Bedouin boy Mahmoud picked up an iron rod and smashed his father's head in. On those low, parched hills, where weeds barely grow and the sun is close and strikes you with the heat of hot coals. It's all as poor as a curse, a corrugated aluminum shack, a few tents, an ass or two, no car, a beaten mother, panicky sisters who lift their arms to protect their faces. And the father, the man who beats them all—his own father, his wife, and his children. For years everyone knew that he abused them but didn't talk about it. Even the police didn't fool with him. It was an internal Bedouin matter, to be dealt with quietly.

There's sometimes a small milk-giving herd by the tents, there on the road between Arad and Beersheba, near the village of Keseifa, which barely looks like a village. My skin crawls just thinking about life in that desert, where there is no corner in which to shelter from the sun or from a violent father. Yet there was life there for eighteen years, from the time the boy was born to the time he took up the rod and struck.

"My father hates me a lot," the boy said to the police inspector immediately after he was arrested. "Yesterday he slugged me when we were arguing about school, and this morning he took an iron rod to me. I grabbed it and gave him back two or three whacks. He fell to the ground." Afterwards they found a knife and a large stone there also, and a lot of blood. "Right after I finished hitting him, I let him go so he'd fall on the ground and I woke up my little sisters and took them out, and I also ran outside and washed my hands and went in the direction of the asphalt, and then I told the police what happened." Patricide is such a severe taboo in Bedouin encampments that there had never been one until this murder. It's not completely clear what the boy murderer's age was at the time. The police inspector's report states that he was nineteen. Abandoned and alone, forever banned, the boy has sat in jail from the moment he turned himself in. Thin and starved by his agonies. When he talks, his handsome face hangs down. He never lifts his eyes to look into the face of a stranger.

There are a few who come to visit him—his mother once every two weeks, his younger brother, the attorney, Grossman, who took the case after the sentencing in the district court, when it was too late to save him.

His mother visited him when he was still incarcerated in Beersheba and she saw the terrible weight on the soul of this boy who had raised his hand against God. Religiously forbidden to kill himself, he was duty bound, when the day came, to emerge from prison and save his family from drowning in its poverty. "He is closed up inside himself," wrote the psychiatrist who visited him in jail for an examination. "He maintains no social contacts. Endlessly tortures himself with his thoughts. His outward behavior is irreproachable. He maintains a clean and neat appearance, does not use drugs, is not involved in acts of violence. Works diligently in the prison workshop and seems to accept his sentence submissively, out of profound feelings of guilt and tribal tradition, according to which he is to be a pariah, forever bearing the mark of Cain on his forehead."

The boy spent his first years in prison in hunger and solitude, swallowing two slices of bread and a glass of milk just to keep himself alive, never eating his fill. At first he slept in a room with twelve drug addicts and other criminals and was paralyzed with fear. He was a dark, smooth-skinned boy, so there was reason to be anxious about what would happen to him in that cell. But the other prisoners also realized that his was a heavy matter and they didn't touch him. To the few who came to visit him he said, "It's better here than at home." It was only when he was transferred to another cell block, away from the addicts, and given a room alone that he became somewhat less high-strung and began to eat.

Only one cousin came to his defense, out of the whole tribe. The cousin is an independent young man who chose to get away from Bedouin life, insular and ossified, with its customs and prohibitions, all the things he had learned to despise. Connected to Israeli culture, disconnected from his tribe, the cousin nevertheless maintained contact with people he loved there. In a letter attached to the attorney's pardon petition to the president, the cousin wrote that he decided to lend a hand when he understood that the boy's fate was sealed. "I don't live in the tribe today, and perhaps it is easier for me to try to help where my brothers have not helped." The tribe's compassion was directed entirely toward the murdered father. Had it been up to the tribe, the boy would be dead. There was not one person who would come to court to speak out about the family's dark past and what impelled the boy to his deed.

The cousin had by chance been in the camp on the morning of the murder. He'd seen a sudden commotion of motor vehicles. The desolate place suddenly buzzed, and a rumor spread that the boy had killed his father. Members of the family came from elsewhere to see the body. The police arrived only afterwards. The story spread like fire in the dry desert prairie over which the huge clan that bears the boy's family name is spread. "It was Ramadan, the month of divine mercy, during which murder is forbidden seven times over," the cousin said, "and all the more so patricide. Apparently something happened between him and his father that we'll never know about. No one there talks, after all."

"This boy," the cousin told me with great compassion, "touched something that had always been hidden, that no one speaks about—that there is horrible abuse inside Bedouin families, but there's no one to turn to. All family problems are concealed. Bedouin *sharaf,* honor, says that it's better for the disgrace to remain within the family, that it not get out onto the street. Even if the problem is a serious one, it's better to hide it, so no one will come in from outside to take care of it." He has no idea where the boy found the courage and the strength to violate that code by himself. He'd never exhibited any violence or temper. He'd always been very closed off and quiet. No one could understand what had happened to him. It could very well have been the accumulation of years of suffering and pain. He saw his father beating his mother, and for the Bedouin the mother is the holy of holies. A child tells everything only to his mother.

The cousin had known the family since he was a boy. They'd always been poor. The grandfather had been poor, one son had died of cancer, one was married and lived in penury with an Arab woman in Khan Yunis in the Gaza Strip. Musa, the father, had always been angry, an eccentric in Bedouin terms, unsuccessful, and subject to attacks of fury. One month he'd work as a guard at one of the factories in Beersheba and then he'd sit at home for a month. A short, stocky man, he'd always complained of back pains, but never had he used his strength to do anything for his family. He had ten children, and the Bedouin boy was the oldest son. For years they lived in a cave. Afterwards they put up a tent in the mountains, then moved down to the foothills. Everyone knew that the father was abusive. He'd make his sons stand all night on one foot, or long hours in the winter rain. Once he threw all his wife's belongings into the fire, including the gold jewelry she'd received from her mother. Another time he beat his wife so badly that she went to the police. Once or twice her brothers came to talk to the father and warn him to stop. Many times he'd kicked her out of the tent and sent her home to her parents. On none of these occasions did the boy raise a hand against his father.

The tent camp was a bad place—miserable, poor, and blasted. Had the boy gone to the police, the tribal sheikh would have silenced the whole affair with a single phone call. There was a conspiracy of silence. And it was convenient for the police—they preferred that the Bedouin deal with such matters themselves. Only such a man's parents or relatives can intervene to prevent abuse. Generally the wife's parents are from the same tribe, and in that case they are liable to support the abuser. Institutions such as the *qadi*, the local Islamic judge and clergyman, can restore children to their mother, but they cannot solve a problem within a family. If a Bedouin social worker who's not from the same tribe shows up, someone will tell him, "If you don't want a broken leg, get out of here." So everything fell on the son himself. He argued with his father on the evening of the murder. It was the time of the Ramadan fast, when people are sometimes tenser and more easily upset. The quiet boy was at least eighteen and had already taken responsibility for the family upon himself. He took his brothers and sisters to school, hauled water, and at the same time prepared for his high school graduation exams.

The father didn't want his son to continue his studies and threatened to pour kerosene over the shack and set it on fire. Amidst the shouting and the anger the younger son fled and went to sleep with the neighbors. Three little sisters who had no other choice went to sleep in the shack's second room. Before they fell asleep the father threatened to kill his son, who was lying beside him. He had an iron rod next to his bed. The boy did not shut his eyes all night out of fear he'd be killed. He lay there with his eyes open waiting for the morning. They awoke at four A.M. to eat the pre-fast Ramadan meal. The father called the boy over and swung the iron rod at him, hitting him above the eye. The boy, overcome by terror, was in a groggy dream state. He grabbed the iron rod, tearing it out of his father's hands and landing three powerful blows on his father, who was still on his bed. "My God, I'm going to kill you now," the father said as he fell.

"There was a knife on the floor, close to both of us, and I was afraid that Father would take it so I grabbed the knife and stuck it in his neck, I don't remember which side," the son testified. After that he picked up a large rock and brought it down on his father's head. According to the pathologist's report, the father apparently died even before the knife and the rock. But the son went on in a blind rage and crushed his father's head with the force of everything that was breaking out

———

in him and which he could no longer control. After he emerged, stumbling and trembling, his little sisters related, he washed his hands and turned himself in.

When the police came, the father was sprawled on his bed, smashed like an insect. The first detective to take testimony from the boy was a member of his tribe. "This is the rock I threw on Father at the end," said the boy, identifying exhibit C, "and this is the iron rod I beat Father with," he said, identifying exhibit A. In the courtroom in Beersheba a court-appointed attorney defended him. The tribe excommunicated him and no one would help. No one mentioned abuse. And the boy did not want to slander his father, so a defense of the kind sometimes used in parricide cases was not made. When the boy testified, he looked at the floor. The judges, who did not go deeply into the case and were unaware of what the boy had been through, wrote in their judgment that "in light of the manner in which he testified and responded, it seems that the defendant is prepared to do or say anything to save his skin." In their blindness they took him for a liar and sentenced him to life in prison.

After the boy had spent three years in prison, a young Israeli combat soldier murdered his father in almost identical circumstances. There was an altercation with an abusive father, after which a family member fled. Father and son were left together in a single room, the son facing his father, who was in bed, and murdering him in a wild fit of rage. In the soldier's trial, the district court wrote that "this is one of the most difficult cases that fate has given us to decide. The uncertainties are among the most difficult that any court ever encounters owing to profoundly conflicting interests: the sanctity of life and the deterrence of the many on the one hand, and the fact that this defendant, as strange as it may sound, needs no punishment, as he atones for his crime each day and each hour as he is compelled to cope with his agonies and his conscience. . . . We could not help but feel a certain sympathy, intertwined with great sorrow, for this young man who was caught, unwillingly, in the tempest of the harsh and turgid relations between his parents, until he made in his heart the horrible decision to do the deed he did . . . to kill the father who sired him. The defendant's distress was real, and there is scant parallel for the void he found himself in."

There was no one to make these observations on behalf of the Bedouin boy. There were no judges with open eyes, nor supportive family members. No one from his tribe came forward with the truth about the father, about the horror of the years that preceded the murder. There were no buddies from the airborne brigade to sit in the courtroom, or newspaper reporters to write commentaries on the deed. The soldier was sentenced to ten years. Another boy who put thirty bullets into his father received six years; a wife and son who used a knife and ax to murder their husband and father were given four and a half years each. Only the Bedouin boy was left to his fate. One day, old and bent, he will return to the dry hills of Keseifa. Though banned by his tribe, he will support his mother and sisters, whom no one will have married because of his crime. He'll bear the sin on his back, in the family tent far from the tribe's camp, to his very last day. I think of the heat there, and of the boy, and I am overcome with a feverish fear, like that which comes over me when I look at a medieval painting of the Judgment Day in which red demons grin as they drag human beings into the fiery pit.

HELLER'S LATE DOCTORATE

AVRAHAM HELLER WAS THE SON of a watchmaker. An old but marvelously clear photograph shows Heller as a boy playing chess in the garden of his parents' home in Lithuania, before he left. There is a table, and chess pieces, and a clock with Hebrew letters under a flowering tree. There are boots on his feet.

At the age of seventeen he went to Berlin to study at the university. When he arrived he didn't know a single person in the strange city. He kept a diary in a thick notebook. On the first night he described himself taking a place to sleep in a miserable room with three beds. In one slept a peddler who spent all day going door to door and at night, in his sleep, squealed like a pig being slaughtered. For thirty marks a month Heller got a bed, coffee in the morning and tea in the evening, saints' pictures on the wall, and a rank odor from the sheets. A few days later he moved into a room of his own. His two Berlin landladies were of different sorts, the first one phlegmatic and unhelpful, her successor aggressive and irritating. In each case there was a cross hanging above his bed, but in that Germany, which was already slouching toward Nazism, he still hadn't felt hatred. He fell in love with a girl with almond eyes and published, in Robert Streicher's journal, a fierce and bitter review of a new poem, "Again Have You Seen the Shortness of Your Reach," by a Hebrew poet named Bialik. At first the student Heller described bitter depression in his diary. Later, when he was accepted into the university and made friends, he was happy. He and his friends rented a bus and drove to Bavaria—"a land of eye-filling beauty," he wrote in his diary. "We climbed mountains and descended into vales and saw forests and cities." For five years he studied, in the final years simultaneously working on his doctoral dissertation on the subject "The Jews of Russia from the March 1917 Revolution to the Present Day." His teachers and professors, Wasmar and Hatch, were fond of him, and when the Nazis came to power, the university remained a protected bubble. Heller's flatmate was a Nazi student who never bothered him. A surviving photograph of the apartment building shows a swastika flag cascading down from the roof. When he went to the neighborhood pub his flatmate would greet him with a Nazi salute. Yet no one interfered with his writing, or told him what to think.

In '34, Heller set down the last words of his 128-

page opus and the dean of the faculty of humanities, Bieberbach, asked Professors Hatch and Wasmar to evaluate the work. Professor Hatch was full of admiration, though he had a few reservations. In his evaluation he wrote that "Avraham Heller is a self-consciously nationalist Jew who supports Zionism. . . . [Nevertheless,] he has mastered the material dispassionately. He worked with great diligence and has made a substantial contribution to the study of Eastern Europe in this period. . . . When it comes down to it, this is an extremely valuable monograph that arrives at interesting conclusions." He noted a few flaws that required correction, but recommended a grade of "praiseworthy." The second reader, Wasmar, endorsed Hatch's comments, but added his own, including: "It would be worth knowing why reactionary circles suffer under the impression that bearded Jews are sympathetic to Bolshevism."

On the fifth of July of the same year, Heller stood for his oral examination before a panel of four professors, from whom he received a grade of "very good." The award of the Ph.D. was dependent only on having 150 copies of his dissertation printed. Professor Hatch wrote to a publisher, extolling the great value of Heller's study, which was "devoid of vengeful sentiments and is entirely scholarly and objective." He recommended that it be printed. A short time later Heller received a first copy of his work from the Marcus Press—a gray bound booklet that remains in his possession to this day.

He was a happy scholar who had completed his studies, had received his doctorate of humanities, and who lived with a girl he loved. But come the winter of '34, Jews began to be harassed on the streets of Berlin and there was a sense of suffocation in the air. As an enthusiastic and restless Zionist, Heller had trouble holding himself back in the face of the coming storm, so he hastily sent a letter to Gimnasia Herzliyya, a high school in Tel Aviv, offering his services as a teacher. Before leaving Berlin he married his girlfriend, a music student named Jutta, and bought two tickets on a boat to Palestine. He did not remain for the official graduation ceremony, which was scheduled to take place at the university in the winter of 1935.

In Tel Aviv, Heller lived on middle-class Rothschild Avenue and began teaching. When the school asked to see his official Ph.D. diploma, he wrote to Berlin and received a quick response—send twenty-four reichs-marks and everything will be taken care of. Heller sent the money, but in January of '36 a short letter signed by Dean Bieberbach arrived in his mailbox like a bomb: "You claim that in 1935 you were awarded a doctoral degree by the faculty of humanities of the University of Berlin. I request that you desist from this imaginary claim. Nor will a doctorate be awarded you in the future, since you clearly are not worthy of bearing any German academic degree. A reexamination of your research has confirmed this fact unambiguously. The faculty, moreover, regrets having allowed you to sit for your doctoral examination."

Heller was so astonished that he immediately sent a letter inquiring into what might possibly have happened. "I suspect that my name has been mistaken for someone else's." He received no reply for the next fifty-six years. He simply lived with the puzzle, far from that Berlin in which everything human had been destroyed, and where everyone denied what he had said yesterday in order to save his job and even his neck. Heller had a classroom and friends and a small family. He made a point of taking his daughter to the zoo on May Day so that she would not take part in the Bolshevik parade, so that her mind would not be corrupted by red ideas. For thirty-seven years Dr. Heller taught thousands of students at Gimnasia Herzliyya, boycotted Germany as all his friends did, and never went back there.

For six months he stubbornly refused to get into the Volkswagen his daughter bought. He went to every demonstration against accepting reparation payments from Germany. In 1961, this time through a lawyer, he once again contacted the university—now located in East Berlin—and demanded his Ph.D. A short time later he received an alternative diploma from the Commissar for the People's Education. The Communists controlled the university then and they didn't like his work, which looked anti-Soviet to them. Years went by and Heller retired, and his wife, Jutta, died after a lengthy illness. He lived in their cozy home, nestled in greenery in an old neighborhood in Ramat Gan, an eighty-year-old man surrounded by books and memories. Then the riddle of the letter he received in 1936 was solved.

A letter arrived at the Heller home in Ramat Gan. It was from a Dr. Ulrich Jancke. He introduced himself as a research assistant in the department of the history of science at Humboldt University—the University of Berlin. Jancke related how, in 1992, while he was searching the university archives for documents relating to his research, he unintentionally discovered a single copy of a doctoral dissertation from 1935, written by a student named Avraham Heller. The dissertation was attached to a thick file of documents, file 791, containing hundreds of pages of correspondence about Heller. Jancke was swept up, as often happens to people who work in archives, and began delving into the intricacies of the case. Thus did an old controversy burst out of the dusty file. There were sentences like "This promises to cause a large-scale slander campaign against Germany"; and "There is a risk that Heller will publicize his claims internationally"; and "The study is a serious affront to Nazi Germany." Jancke, the research assistant, had discovered what transpired in Berlin after Heller moved to Palestine. A great ruckus over a modest dissertation by a Jew in Tel Aviv. Professors and deans had trembled in a country that aspired to conquer the world.

It turned out that in December 1935, when Heller was already teaching in Tel Aviv and waiting for his diploma to arrive from Berlin, the university's humanities faculty received a letter from one Dr. Graefe, a man who always signed his letters "Heil Hitler." He was director of the Institute for the Scientific Study of the Soviet Union, an institution of the type that flourished under the Nazis. "We have just received Avraham Heller's book on the situation of the Jews in Russia and have determined that this is a work of Jewish propaganda of the worst type. Its purpose is to contradict Adolf Hitler's fundamental view of Marxism-Bolshevism as a political tool of Judaism. The Führer has expressed, unmistakably, in his own book, his consciousness that Soviet Russia is ruled by an international gang of foreign race. The Jew's attempt to contradict the Führer's views through this work of propaganda can only be considered an attack on the National Socialist world view. It is worth noting that this research was encouraged by Professor Otto Hatch, the infamous Bolshevik ideologue, and by Professor Wasmar. The fact that a Jew is allowed to submit such a work as a Ph.D. dissertation at the University of Berlin—in 1935—is so shocking that I am speechless. We expect that the university will want to expunge this stain by immediately revoking its grant of a degree to Mr. Heller."

Copies of the letter were immediately sent to the foreign affairs office of the Nazi Party, to the Ministry of Propaganda, to the Ministry of Education, to Gauleiter Julius Streicher, to the Office for the Advancement of Nonfiction Literature, to the party's examination board for the protection of Nazi books, to the Anti-Comintern, to the university's rector, and to the chairman of the Nazi Student Association.

The letter exploded across the university, setting off a furious fever of self-purification and denial. File 791 is full of dismay. Two days after receiving Graefe's letter, Dean Bieberbach wrote to the minister of science that he had ordered the university library to retrieve all copies of the work that had already been lent out. The professor who had commended the work, Hatch, was already at home, having been expelled from the university. Professor Wasmar apologized and explained that Heller had, in fact, never been a student of his. Wasmar nevertheless defended his recommendation, claiming that Heller's dissertation was "a deadly critique of Bolshevism, and is likely to make a great impression in Germany and other countries precisely because it was written by a Zionist Jew. . . . Of all the currents of thought popular among the Jews," wrote Wasmar, "Zionism seems to me to be the most acceptable, insofar as ridding the countries of Europe of their Jews, as Nazism advocates, could be most easily accomplished via Zionism."

Wasmar recommended against revoking Heller's Ph.D. degree, since this "would likely increase his popularity overseas." The snowball that Heller had unwittingly created continued to gain momentum. A week after his first letter, Graefe restated his claim that "there is a danger that Heller will publish his denial of Hitler's thesis internationally and back it up with a doctorate approved by the University of Berlin. The university should challenge the grant of the degree, since otherwise it will trigger a huge slander campaign against Germany." The panicked dean quickly sent Heller the only letter he would receive in the matter, the one that had made him suspect that his name had been mixed up with someone else's. Had Heller only known what power was attributed to him and what a danger he represented to the Third Reich's public image.

In the spring of 1936, seven honorable but terrified Berlin professors were shut up in the dean's room, where together they drafted a statement declaring that "Avraham Heller's book seriously harms Germany's interests. . . . Heller has shown by this study that he is not worthy of bearing a German academic degree." University Rector Krieger and the dean of the faculty of theology, Stultzenberg, were there, as was the acting dean of the law faculty, Professor Amga, and the acting dean of the faculty of medicine, Professor Friedrich. Also present were Bieberbach of humanities and Bieberbaum from the veterinary school, and Littmeier, the university's provost. Lying on the heavy desk was a written opinion they had solicited from another professor, according to which the dissertation was a serious attack on the Führer and Germany. All copies of the dissertation were collected and destroyed, including the one Dr. Hatch had taken home with him. All the professors involved were reprimanded by the minister of science, and each one replied with a letter in which he blamed his error on a misunderstanding, or on a colleague. German precision required the acknowledgment of the fact that Heller had been awarded his degree, but a contorted formula was employed to retract what could not be denied. Luckily, Heller himself, the cause of all the excitement, was beyond the Nazis' strangling grasp.

When Jancke raised his head from the documents in the archives, he began searching for Heller. He placed an ad in a German-Israeli newspaper and discovered

Heller, elderly but alive and well in Ramat Gan. Jancke sent him the material and demanded that the university reinstate its recognition of Heller's degree. Six months later, Heller's name was formally cleared and a certificate was issued marking the fiftieth anniversary of the awarding of his Ph.D. One hundred forty copies of his dissertation were printed for distribution. "While these measures cannot repair the injustice done to you, they express the university's willingness to compensate for and confront its past," they wrote to him.

When I came to Heller's home, the aged teacher repeated in astonishment that at the time they had thought that "my intention was to poison Germany with my doctorate." Heller was invited to Berlin for a formal ceremony in which his belated doctorate would be presented to him. When Heller declined, Professor Link notified him from Berlin that if that was the case, they intended to come to his house and conduct the ceremony there.

A day before the ceremony, a car from the German Embassy arrived in the old Ramat Gan neighborhood to locate the house, and on the day of the ceremony the Germans waited on the street for a long while in order to enter at precisely the appointed time, hoping, it would seem, to get it right nearly sixty years later. They had forty new copies of the old dissertation with them. The first page was a foreword by a Professor Duerrkopf. "When we bring before the scholarly public a dissertation written fifty-seven years ago, the unusual delay demands an explanation," it began.

THE DEAD COMPANY

NEBULOUSLY, AS THROUGH A SCREEN OF SMOKE, I call up the last scenes from the Bir Temadeh army camp in the heart of the Sinai Desert. Sergeant Tzofar Zahavi stands there counting heavy machine guns in a hot tent full of weapons. I sign off on the company's guns and gear before driving off to be discharged without looking back. That was in the summer of '73, when I left Armored Battalion 46. We didn't yet know, those of us who left the army in August, how lucky we were, finishing up our military service a few weeks before the deadly October eruption that would sweep away tanks and toss them in the air with the same ease that sandstorms whirl thorny acacia bushes. A few months later, after the war, Tzofar Zahavi would appear to me in a dream; here he comes, approaching my parents' house in Tel Aviv. Walking slowly, wounded and bloody, stumbling down narrow Zlatopolsky Street. I run out to him to support and embrace this beloved friend, who I already knew by then had been killed by a direct hit in the commander's cupola of his tank. Tzofar, Tzofar, the name returns, echoing from the dead. In the journey I made into my memory, to my friends, to the missing and the saved, wherever I went, Tzofar's name was always there. Sergeant Tzofar, the winsome kibbutz boy, whose *s*'s whistled through the space between his front teeth, who remains alive and loved in my memory even twenty years later. His name was the end of the rope you hold on to to reach the opening of the cave.

The years had covered that memory with a scab, but the scab was so brittle that the first question opened it and bared everything. As if people had just been waiting to be asked about that time, the war lying within them, a great disaster that had been visited upon the friends whom they'd loved with all their souls, that had charred their lives. One sergeant ran away to California and another seldom sleeps at night, a third lives on tranquilizers and panics every time an envelope from the military appears in his mailbox. Some of them had families and broke them up, and they recall the Sinai years with the feeling sometimes left behind by a tempestuous intimate relationship in which there is love alongside hatred, and a powerful urge to escape.

All that will be told here took place in the tankland of the Sinai Desert, an enormous, baking expanse of sand cut off from Israel just as a Foreign Legion base in the Sahara is cut off from life in Paris. This tankland, its life, its war, and its cities of soldiers, is dead. It is now buried under Egyptian sand and comes to life only in the memories of those who remain. The voice from the the past sounds like a rusty tank turret turning, after being shot at for twenty years with its dead and desiccated crew inside. The creaking of ghosts.

I begin my memory in the time before the war, during the nearly three years when my armored company was stationed in Sinai, facing the enemy, close to the Suez Canal shore. The company trained, eyed the other side, and had no conception of what awaited it. When I speak of the company I mean fifty-six boys, all of whom knew all the others and most of whom were killed within a ten-minute tank drive of each other. The company lived on the battalion's base, which was made up of aluminum and plastic structures put up on the dust plains of Bir Temadeh—a yellow-gray place where no green plants were to be seen, except for the weeds sprouting from the soapy water that flowed out of the showers. A hot place, desolate and suffocating.

South of there, on platforms of dust at the foot of a range of rocky hills, we put new soldiers, armored corps trainees who had just arrived from Israel, through training as exhausting as the inferno. Most of them were frightened high school kids; Sinai was a doomsday land that cut them off from their old lives. They went home once every five weeks. That was the only rest except for brief Saturdays on base, when they collapsed on their beds in the hot corrugated metal sheds and woke up on Saturday night to return to their tanks. More than once, I remember, these young soldiers who had been thrown into the desert had their spirits broken a bit more than was necessary. There were incidents like when a despairing soldier slammed an eleven-pound hammer down on his foot and was sent to the hospital for two months' observation. Or another case, in which a new crewman killed himself while on guard duty at the base's gate. He shot himself in the chest and remained sitting there, dead, on the punctured guard's chair, while the entire battalion tried vainly to locate the source of the gunfire. The nights were short and the days long. In the space of three months, the scared high school kid was meant to undergo a mental process that would turn him into a battle-ready tank fighter. At the end of the training period, heavy tank carriers would arrive and bring the brigade, with its tanks and huge quantities of equipment, to the armored outposts on the canal, to sit there, defenders of the homeland facing the invisible Egyptian enemy.

The company's bunker, code-named "Vatican," was a huge underground concrete structure concealed beneath a thick slab that protected it from shelling. According to the Doctrine, the bunker would, in time of trouble, send impervious armored companies to the canal shoreline. The Egyptian enemy, on the other side of the canal's blue stripe of water, was an object of jest and a source of rumors about rotting food, whores, and low morale. Memories of the Egyptian rout in the Six Day War, when defeated soldiers straggled through the desert, barefoot and dying of thirst, floated in the air like promises of a swift and easy engagement if war should come. The battalion was responsible for a huge zone fifty miles long, which it covered without shifting its tanks. Sometimes, at night, the electronic radar that kept track of things would detect rapid movements. In the morning there would be the tracks of people who had crossed to the Israeli side and returned to Egypt, though none were ever intercepted. Something was happening, but it did not impinge on our complacency.

Egyptians in the pay of Israeli intelligence met with their operators by the Bitter Lakes. There was no mood of war in the air, I was told by Colonel N., who was then the battalion's intelligence officer and now serves in the intelligence unit that deciphers aerial photographs. The heat and the distance imbued us with a smug fatigue, and it seemed as if the exhausting tank-crew training maneuvers would go on forever in anticipation of a war that would never come. "We saw the Egyptians putting up high earth embankments. They trained breaking through earthworks right before our eyes, and we were unfazed," he would recall. And I remembered how once, in a talk our regimental commander had with the soldiers, tank gunner Noyes got up and asked a question. Noyes was a sharp-eyed and skeptical Tel Aviv high school graduate who had not yet allowed the military to dull his senses. He asked about the Egyptian earthworks and how we would operate against Egyptian infantry. The colonel waved his hand dismissively. In his memory were images of flaccid, fat Egyptians, the caricature of the Arab we had grown up on, in their grungy trenches. Noyes sat back down and fell silent. He would be killed at the bitter battle of the Chinese Farm.

In the winter of '71/'72 we were thirteen tank crews in a company led by a stern officer who pursued his soldiers even in their nightmares. He sometimes appeared in my dreams as well, running after me with a drawn knife in his hand. In the company latrines, corrugated metal shacks erected above septic barrels, bitter soldiers recorded, as they crouched to crap, the curses they sought to inflict on him. The company commander was a young captain from an old-style patriotic family, all of whose sons had gone to military boarding schools and then on to command combat vessels, from submarines to tanks. We were terrified of him and we eventually became his sworn enemies, even when we were commanders ourselves. He was as strict and professional as a Prussian officer, imbued with a fierce belief that the moment absolute control of his men's lives slipped out of his grasp, everything would collapse around him. He kept a distance from all of us, and would approach only to mete out a reprimand or punishment. In those moments he would bare his white teeth in a frozen smile, a terror that could not be faced. Until his death in his tank on the Golan Heights he observed the tank regulations as if they were a codex supreme over all else. Even in his final hours he lay tires under his tank treads when he had to cross an asphalt road.

Sometimes in soldiers' collective memories, images remain of commanders of this type, officers who took too much liberty for themselves. At the Bir Temadeh tank base, a tiny spot in a sea of sand, our company commander was like the merciless captain of a whaling ship, believing that no one but God oversaw his actions. Above him, on this remote base, stood only the battalion commander—an older officer from the airborne brigade, a gentleman with a chiseled profile who always felt embarrassed and clueless next to professional tank men.

To this day there are officers who miss the freedom that commanders had then in Sinai—freedom that included huge areas for maneuvers, plentiful ammunition and fuel, no furloughs, and no oversight or supervision of any sort. No concerned parents or intrusive newspaper reporters ever showed up. In clouds of dust we would go out into the field with our tanks for a week—with all our gear, soldiers, and weapons, accompanied by a technical crew. Behind us there was always the first sergeant's command car with clattering aluminum pots that let sand into the food, supplying all our needs in a place where only an American spy satellite bothered to watch us. Standing alongside the company commander, and more or less obedient to him, were the platoon commanders, and alongside them, we, the tank commanders. The young officers I remember from that time included Perel, who would be badly wounded in his face in the war and who would many years later be elected mayor of Safed. There was also First Lieutenant Zucker, an amiable hulk who liked to drip burning candle wax on drowsing tank commanders and throw darts at soldiers. There was the good officer Laner, the only one who put some fear into the captain, being a general's son. And there was the well-mannered officer Broide from Tel Aviv, who would be killed while trying to save the crew of a blasted tank. The platoon sergeants were Kugel, Braz, Mintz, and me. The first three had no fathers. Avi Mintz was a rosy-faced country boy, diligent as a farmer and innocent as a lamb, who always fell victim to the captain's wrath.

From the distance of time it seems to me that we were always out in the huge training areas that spread to the south of Bir Temadeh. We were always racing over some dusty end of the world that looked just like the other dusty end of the world where we had halted the week before. We always erected, like a pointless ritual, the two tents for technical crew and the first sergeant, the parking spaces for the someone who would never arrive, the field motor pool with the sawed-off half-barrel of fuel and half-barrel for spent cartridges. We erected an Israeli flag and an armored corps flag on a territory of nothing—a temporary miniature base around which we trained our tank crews, attacking imaginary positions, crushing them with tank treads, shooting high-explosive rounds at the rusty skeletons of Egyptian tanks that, at a range of about a mile, symbolized enemy tanks, and spraying imaginary infantry with machine-gun fire.

By day the company moved with the edginess that permeated all life there, and at night we drove without lights, shooting at targets set aflame before nightfall. In the ubiquitous dust, all that was visible to the eye was the phosphorescent mark at the end of the antenna on the tank in front of you. There was always the same chaos in this congealed darkness, deriving from the gloom and the inevitable eclipse of rationality that takes place in armored units when the contours of the land disappear. It never crossed anyone's mind that the battalion's critical test would come at night.

During those few days we actually spent at the base, when we engaged in the tedious maintenance of our tanks, the company's soldiers went to the mess hall collapsing under the weight of machine guns and iron bars, fire extinguishers and other pieces of equipment they were forced to carry as punishment for every soldierly infraction or piddling sin of omission. In the winter they tramped about wrapped in coats filthy with diesel fuel and grease, like seabirds mired in an oil spill. In the summer they stank from a week without washing. And they were halted again and again on their way to their meals until they sang out joyfully enough to satisfy their commanders. They always looked forlorn, a perpetually chastised company, and by the time they sat down to eat, their time was up, so they hastily grabbed a slice of bread and ran to their tanks. There was no time for anything but the tanks. Free time was a four-letter word. The captain would sometimes lie in ambush at night by the forlorn showers in order to catch any soldier who tried to slip in there for a moment. There are soldiers who believe to this day that he opened their letters and listened in on the telephone calls they made from the office.

At night, not a single soldier was allowed to go to the barracks before the completion of the tank maintenance routine, that Sisyphean task. They tightened treads and cleaned the turret, washed down the machine guns in a mixture of gasoline and diesel fuel, and labored to get rid of dust in a place where dust storms were the rule. When they thought they had finished, toward midnight, the commander would come and find some flaw, and the work began anew. There was always a screw that had not been tightened or a bullet cartridge that had been forgotten on the turret floor. Sometimes, when the time for morning inspection arrived, some of the crews were still in their tanks, and day was joined to day with no reprieve. They stood at inspection, swaying in that dim dawn Bir Temadeh hour when they were roused from the beds they had slept on in their grimy clothes, or were called from their tanks.

Is my memory misleading me in its selection of scenes, as it so often does? Was it really all so harsh and depressing, I keep asking myself and my friends. Sometimes I also remember other moments. The intoxicating fragrance that wafted upwards when, in a wadi, the tank treads ran over desert scrub that had not yet dried out. Lying around doing nothing alongside a tank that wouldn't start, while the rest of the company went off for maneuvers. Or, afterwards, in a different company, at a different outpost, in a place where the dust had become soft sand, a soldier projecting old movies in the hot concrete corridor, with the tanks resting under camouflage nets like old, retired circus elephants.

A year was ripped out of my life under that hard captain. Then I transferred to become master sergeant in Gaon's company. He was a good-looking graduate of a military school who drove as if he were starring in a Hollywood movie about a tank company commander. He always wore an immaculate uniform that seemed to fit his slender frame perfectly, and he tapped his cigarettes on the box before lighting them. He was strict with his soldiers but fair. Only after his death, in a tank at the Chinese Farm, did we discover that he had sent moving letters to his girlfriend, with sentences like: "I'm a man in a soldier's costume, confined inside a madman's cloak." The words were set to music in a song called "Don't Cry for Me, Girl," which became a cult hit among young people.

New commanders came to Bir Temadeh to train the soldiers that poured in from Israel. After two years in the battalion we were a solid group that could handle the toughest of captains. But back in the city, when I arrived for short furloughs, there was no longer anyone I could talk to. In July I completed my three years and I left the battalion and the desert together with Sergeants Kugel, Braz, and Mintz. Three months before the war, I went through a short course to retrain on Centurion tanks, and in the war itself I was a twenty-one-year-old reservist fighting on the Golan Heights alongside people I didn't know and whose fate didn't touch my heart. In hard moments, when death was close by, such as the battle on the peak of Mount Hermon, I thought of my friends in Sinai. I was still linked by the aorta to the company fighting on the southern front, a day's drive away through the sands.

Years later I am forced to tie together threads and testimonies in order to form a picture of the battle I was no longer present for.

At two in the afternoon on Yom Kippur in 1973, a few minutes before the war, when peril was already in the air, so I was told, there was no one in the shacks of the Bir Temadeh base except for the soldier doing his shift at the radio receiver. Everything was quiet and orderly, and the emergency crates contained only maps of the Egyptian side of the canal. The battalion intelligence officer had taken a look, along with the colonel, at the latest stomach-curdling aerial photographs of huge Egyptian forces on the other side of the water. Worried, he'd run off to the adjacent regimental base to prepare code maps of the Israeli side of the canal as well. All the armored company's soldiers were packed into the large aluminum mess hall, where rows of wooden benches had been arranged. They were waiting for final orders before descending to the canal on our tracks at three in the afternoon to reinforce the outposts there. They conceived of reinforcement in terms of the "Dovecote" plan, which we'd grown up on.

As the soldiers listened to the colonel, there were suddenly tremendous explosions. The building, constructed out of light materials, quaked, and the operations sergeant, who had been alone outside, tore in, screaming that they were bombing the base, that Egyptian planes were coming down on the nearby runway. There was a riot. Everyone panicked and pushed out the only door. Sergeant Yakobowitz and Sergeant Tzofar shouted to break the windows and soldiers grabbed benches and pounded out the panes. Everyone jumped out and ran to the tanks. The Egyptian planes passed overhead and fired machine guns without hitting any of the runners. The girls asked, "What about us?" because they didn't have a tank to carry them out of that God-awful chaos. Soldiers shouted at them to run to the old trenches by the fences.

One hundred and forty-four boys belonging to three companies climbed on their tanks and opened the 24-volt switch. The electricity flowed and activated the hydraulic turret motors. The radio sputtered, broadcasting directives about the order of movement, and Sergeant Yakobowitz remembered too late that the Yom Kippur box with the food for those who were not fasting was in his room, along with the cigarettes. Lieutenant Zatorsky drove his tank into the base, breaking a holy writ of the old life, which at that very moment had lost all meaning. He avidly ran over the fences and green posts and whitewashed stone markers that were part of the cult of the armored corps and drove straight up to the room and grabbed the cigarettes. No one had yet realized where they were going, and no one had any conception of how bloody it would be, or that by the next morning many of them would be dead or missing.

The air was thick with the noise of a tank battalion

in motion. The deep rumble of thirty-six 750-horsepower Continental engines punctuated by desperate hydraulic screeches. The endless static of radio receivers being switched on. The mumbling and whispering and shouting of the battalion radio network and the creaking of the treads getting on their way. The sound of the breaker bars under the tanks stretching and the bangs of hatches being closed and the rattle of the technical crew's half-track. Final cries of farewell before all communication would be conducted on the radio and in accordance with battle protocol. And amidst all this, each individual crewman getting himself settled in his little chamber, adjusting the height of the commander's chair, opening the cannon's breech, preparing a belt of ammunition by the machine guns just in case, and getting a few shells into easy reach. They rode together in a huge cloud of dust, moving in the direction of the canal. Egyptian Suhoi fighters still dove down very low over the battalion, the heat of their jet engines blowing a thunder that drowned out the sound of the tanks. Some of the tank commanders fired their machine guns at them. No one hit, or was hit—it was all like a video game, without a drop of blood.

For a while we drove on the road, galloping along in battalion formation in the direction of the canal, the radio issuing warnings of enemy planes. Suddenly, at a point that had once been in the heart of Israeli territory, Sager antitank missiles started flying and foreign tracks appeared on the hilltops. Yakobowitz remembers that the sight was so surprising that an order was given not to shoot because they might be ours. "But that thing on the hilltop, which turned out to be an Egyptian APC, fired and hit a spot just below the company, and immediately eleven shells went out. All the tanks fired, and the thing disappeared in an instant in a firestorm." The intelligence officer remembers that it was almost four o'clock when the first company identified enemy vehicles, and everyone was in shock, because it was 20 miles inside Israeli territory and it was already known that outposts had fallen to the enemy. Evening, with a glowing moon, came very quickly, as it does in the fall, and then came the longest night. The regimental intelligence officer, who would later be killed while on recon, received a report from the battalion intelligence officer that the Egyptians were crossing all along the canal. The battalion maintenance officer remembers that he drove with the technical crew behind the tanks in the old half-tracks, and suddenly passed by camouflaged tanks beside which soldiers in commando uniforms stood—"and we didn't grasp right away that we'd already reached the Egyptians!"

Everything was all mixed up, foe and friend, and the Egyptians were in everything. What began as a unified battalion charge aimed at tossing off a few Egyptian tanks soon broke down into battles by companies, and then by individual tanks. Each tank on its own. There were those who got stuck and those who were sent alone to clean out an outpost that had been occupied, and there were those sent to rescue those who had gotten stuck. "There were a lot of inquiries after that war,"

Lieutenant Zilberberg told me, "and I saw how hard it was to get a clear picture of what happened. Even when you listen to the same crew that was together for the whole war, on the same tank, you get several versions. The gunner and the loader, the commander and the driver had different points of view, and over time each one constructs a different picture for himself. Some things get forgotten and others get etched in the memory. You have to understand that the problem is the first night—the chaos. We lost twelve tanks then. The whole company simply went."

In the winter of 1994, Sergeant Yakobowitz got up one morning and found his hand frozen and numb. More than twenty years after that same clear night following Yom Kippur, an Egyptian bullet that had hit his hand returned to torment him. He was standing with his company on the top of a sandy range of hills, firing his cannon, when he saw a dark man running toward his tank. A few tanks fired at the runner before they saw that it was Nehemia, who'd fled from a tank that had been surrounded by Egyptians. From the moment they'd made contact with the Egyptians, at four P.M., the tanks had moved forward and back, advanced and retreated, reached outposts and left them. Here and there damaged tanks began getting stuck and remaining behind as the company moved on. Sergeant Nisanhaus, so the company recalls to this day, received from one of the officers command of a tank with an electrical problem. He drove it a bit and then got stuck, without a radio and without transmission, close to the canal. He was a goner. Arik Yakobowitz was sent to look for Nisanhaus and rescue him. At that time no one knew that the crew had been killed and that Nisanhaus had fallen into the hands of the Egyptians. They took him prisoner after blinding him in one eye with a rifle butt. A mile and a half after racing to their rescue, Yakobowitz's tank itself ran into an Egyptian ambush. It was in a little sand canyon and the Egyptians opened up on him from every direction. He ordered the loader to prepare ammunition and started squeezing off 105-mm shells at a range of 50 yards like a sharpshooter in a western.

Yakobowitz screamed over the company frequency that he'd fallen into an ambush and was in deep trouble. The entire company heard his shouts, along with the orders he was shouting over the internal radio to the driver, to drive fast, not to stop. When you hit the external radio switch on your helmet, the entire company can hear your tank's internal radio.

It was dark and the driver was stuck in the dunes, and the tank had stopped. Arik had taken two bullets in his arm and was shouting to his driver: "Back! Back!" But then the tank's shroud got stuck in the tread and halted it. In the end they got out by the skin of their teeth and retreated to the company—and Nisanhaus went with the Egyptians to the other side of the canal. A new company, inexperienced, had been caught, on its own territory, in hellfire from every direction, in a chaos filled with the screams of overrun outposts and lost tanks, of curses and supplications and people running around, blazing tanks and tanks swallowed up by the darkness. The Egyptians shot Sager missiles and sometimes flamethrowers and even climbed up on tanks that still had their crews inside.

The captain reported that he'd gotten stuck and asked for someone to pull him out, but his voice grew fainter as he tried to direct the rescuers, until it went entirely silent. Cries for help came from other tanks that had been left on their own. Lieutenants Bugler and Broide, who had also gone to Nisanhaus's aid, disappeared. Broide's tank went silent, but toward dawn the tank's driver began talking on the radio: "Broide's gone," he said, "and I'm wounded. Save us. I don't want to die." He said things that remain in the men's memory to this day. When the driver fell silent, the remaining crewman spoke. He reported that the Egyptians were coming at them and that he was shooting what he had. The flash of his desperate gunfire lit up the black sky, and another tank was sent there. But a Sager missile hit and wounded the commander, and the last crew member fell silent as well.

Now it was the voice of Captain Efron that led on the radio. Whoever keeps his cool in the midst of chaos always stands out, like another officer we had known, Ploznik, who saved a tank in a minefield. He leaned nonchalantly on the shroud and smoked a cigarette while the Egyptians were surrounding him. First Lieutenant Mazar also helped save another outpost, until he was hit in the eye. And our Tzofar, the boy we loved, raced along the canal, between the outposts, to save a friend's tank. He was imperturbable under fire and a great navigator, as if he had been born in the quicksandy stretches between the outposts, and not in green Ein Harod.

Standing, with half his body outside so he could see, Tzofar directed his driver, Delrahim, amid the barbed-wire fences, the earthworks, and the narrow roads. But he got stuck at a turn in the road and couldn't lower the cannon to fire. The Egyptians were so close by the earthworks that Tzofar pelted them with grenades that he had in boxes in the turret. Delrahim heard his voice on the radio but it suddenly went silent. He lifted the driver's hatch and saw the two crewmen on the turret and Tzofar on fire in the commander's cupola. They were pouring water on him to put him out and tried to pull him out but without success. A missile had hit him directly in the neck and had also severed the radio antenna. Heavy fire was directed at the orphaned tank, because it was close to an outpost the Egyptians had already taken.

The two turret men went down to hide in an old railroad car left there from 1967 and Delrahim crouched beside the tank. "All of Tzofar's blood ran down the turret and dripped on me, I'll never forget that." Dr. Delrahim tells me about the incident in a quiet white room of his clinic. One eye is blind and his face is taut, as if he were under interrogation. "Since then I have memories all the time. Every little noise opens all my wounds. I'm so short-tempered, I don't even have patience for my children." He was taken prisoner at the foot of the tank. The Egyptians tossed a grenade inside and set the tank on fire, and they beat Delrahim almost to death, but an officer got him out of there. Stunned, his eye torn, he was dragged away and returned to Israel thirty-seven days later.

I spend hours staring at the testimony I've taken, pages packed with feverish handwriting. How strange it is to read about what happened to people you knew so well, in places you spent years learning how to fight in, and then when it happened you were so far away from there. Can all the memories and sights be tied into a readable account of that night? I glance at the material, then walk away from my desk. I rest and come back again, disturbed by the chaos, and type a few lines. I find that those friends who remain alive have a powerful desire to return to the canal, if only for just a moment. To return to the past in order to assuage the hurt— now, when we know the location of every lost tank, and how close the rescue party was to saving it when it gave up the search and turned back.

A day after I telephoned the California home of former sergeant Yefet in the town of Mount Vellore he called me, at night. "Since we spoke a parade of ghosts has been going by me," he said. "All the demons have come out." Other friends I spoke to found they couldn't sleep. Dr. Delrahim told me about his dream of returning for one day to the place where Tzofar had been killed and where the two other crewmen had been left in the rusty iron railroad car that had been parked there. "I can't forgive myself for not telling the Egyptians about them. Maybe they would have been taken prisoner like me and saved." Tank commander B lives on tranquilizers. Yakobowitz sees the wounded before him every day. The three officers Zilberberg, Ira, and Ram took advantage of an agreement made with the Egyptians immediately after the war and returned several times to the field to look for the lost tanks. Even more than the tank commanders, the officers feel responsible still, for the fate of the missing men. In the years after the war they were pursued on occasion by a grieving father who had discovered that his son had been abandoned alive. They had told him that his son had been killed on the spot, but later, when his son's body was returned, he discovered that it was bandaged, and he had no peace of mind from that day on.

After the war the officers went back, together with men from the military rabbinate, which collected the remains of the dead. They entered the territory with Egyptian consent, equipped with aerial photographs. They found Lieutenant Broide's lost tank in the dunes a mile from the company's position, on the spot from which he had reported and fallen silent. The tank was charred and without bodies. Lieutenant Bugler's tank was at the very edge of the water, and the presumption is that after the commander was killed the deathly panicked driver drove on, stopping only on the bank of the canal, like the last run of a slaughtered chicken. At the entrance to what had been the Lituf outpost, they found Tzofar's tank and a grave the Egyptians had dug by the treads. Here and there the officers found temporary graves by tanks, the body of a crewman under a tank, partial remains, pieces of equipment, a crew assignment form. Next to one burnt tank they found a dead soldier's dog tags in a glass jar. The searchers saw how a company of Egyptian soldiers could move, in the space of hours, a dune that had entirely covered an Israeli tank for months.

Toward dawn after the first night the battalion entered lager formation and then returned again to battle. In the morning, an Israeli Phantom jet swooped down on two of the company's tanks, thinking they were Egyptian. The thunder of an 800-pound bomb flipped one of the tanks over, tearing the turret off the body of the tank and leaving it upside down in the sand. Two crewmen got out and fled. Lieutenant Shmuelowitz, a man six feet tall, was left stuck in the upended turret, trapped between the commander's dome and the ceiling, curled up like an embryo with the cannon pressing into him from the side. He was curled up like that for hours, certain his end had come, and when he was finally rescued he just muttered strange things. In the rescue aircraft that flew him back to Israel he kept repeating, in shock, his name and rank, convinced that he had been taken prisoner by the Egyptians. The tank's driver, who remained in his chamber, heard Egyptians outside his tank half the night, and when they went away he found a full can of water and walked for almost two days, until he caught up with the company.

The company's battles with the Egyptians continued for three days, until the battalion went down to rearm and reorganize. It was only then that everyone suddenly realized how few remained from the battalion that had set out on Saturday with all its tanks. At that time many members of the company who had been discharged before the war or who had transferred to other units were already fighting in other places. Many continued to fall. Not far from the Chinese Farm, Lieutenant Alfasi found himself flying from his tank as it took a direct hit. He lay as if dead for two days in territory swarming with Egyptians, thrown on a pile of Israeli bodies that the Egyptians had made at the side of the road. At night he gathered up his courage and went on his own toward a group of tanks he saw close by. One of them had its motor running and the radio worked in another, but the crews had disappeared. He found something to eat, called out on the radio to nowhere, and only a day later managed to rendezvous with an Israeli force towing a damaged pontoon bridge.

The tank commanders from the August enlistment, Kugel and Mintz, found themselves in the same reserve force that went out to attack an Egyptian outpost in the central sector. Mintz's tank took a direct hit and went up in flames. Mintz and his crew were killed and their bodies remained in the field for a long time.

The battalion was battered, but on the fourteenth of October a great chance came to take revenge for the first night and restore some of their lost confidence. A long-range lookout placed on a high cliff identified the approach of an Egyptian regimental column. The battalion situated its remaining tanks on the hills and constructed a classic armored ambush. It destroyed the

Egyptian regiment, which had entered its valley of slaughter and could not escape. Later that same day a phosphorus shell hit the colonel's tank, wounding him and burning up Operations Officer Uri Pundak, a bright Tel Aviv boy who had come up through the ranks.

Pundak was taken from the turret burned black and looking unconscious, but as they bore him away on a stretcher, a man who knew him from school heard him calling his name and spoke with him. A helicopter took him from there, already dying, to a hospital in Tel Aviv. The battalion, which continued without its commander, reached kilometer marker 101 and stopped there to rehabilitate. It looked as if the terror had passed and quiet had come, but on the last day of 1973, when a group of officers was standing to the side by the company, an officer was playing around with the Kalashnikov submachine gun he had taken from an Egyptian body and shot the war's last deadly bullet. At that time, when death had become the company's permanent companion, people sometimes shot out in all directions as if they had forgotten the safety rules. The bullet that escaped from the rifle hit Lieutenant Schecter in the forehead. Mortally wounded, he died in the helicopter on the way to the hospital. The officer who fired the shot was not tried. They needed every soldier and they remembered his courage during the war.

Slowly, rumors about the company began making their way to me, as I fought in the north, far from there. Who had died and what the men had been through. Most of the rumors were transmitted, like the beat of tom-toms, via army transport points where soldiers who were going down to Sinai encountered those coming up to the Golan. Only then did I learn that Tzofar had been killed, and with him Pundak and Broide, Mintz and Gaon, and other soldiers I had known. In the platoon tent, on a snowy Syrian hill, I dreamed the dream in which the dead Tzofar Zahavi came to my parents' home. That was one of those dreams that do not dissolve the next day but rather join one's stock of memories as a solid piece of reality.

A year after the war, on the day before Independence Day, which is Israel's Memorial Day, I went to visit the parents of some of my friends who had been killed. Mintz's mother's house stood in the middle of their orange grove. She was streaked with tears even as she emptied a crate of yellow grapefruit into our car before we went. Everything was so alive, shivering, and full of pain. The father of the dead officer Broide interrogated us on what exactly had happened there, and he seemed so self-possessed. At Ein Harod, Tzofar's father, a small man, shrunken by calamity, led us to his son's grave, on which he had erected some kind of black sculpture. It was dim in the cemetery copse, and I never could make out what that sculpture was. But I remember the scar that crossed the father's face, caused by a bullet from an Arab ambush, forty years before his son's death in another war.

They told me that the mother of the dead Sergeant Noyes hadn't left her home since she learned of his death, but I didn't dare visit her. Broide's father died a short while after the war, and Tzofar's father followed him, as did Gaon's. There was a period in which grieving fathers were dying at almost the same pace that their sons had disappeared during the war.

"Evening, and everything is so sad," the operations clerk Irit Ya'akobi wrote to a friend from the brigade. "It's so sad for me. In all you do or say, you feel the absence of the fallen. You can't believe that they won't ever be again." She was a wild-haired, barefoot kibbutz girl, and the war took several people in the battalion whom she had loved very much. When she completed her army service she returned to Kibbutz Ma'agan Michael. In the October of the war's second anniversary, after meeting several of her old friends at memorial ceremonies, she disappeared from the kibbutz. It was a week later that a member of the kibbutz found her naked body in the avocado orchard. Her clothes were hanging on the trees around her. She was murdered in circumstances that have never been solved, walking in the dark from Ma'agan Michael to the bus stop on the road. Like a late blow of fate just as the memory of the war began to go dim.

To this day some of the men remain very close, and among them there are even two business partnerships. The officers Ira and Alfasi set up a software firm called Applicom and share a floor of luxurious offices—but sometimes they have a hard time talking to each other. Zilberberg has a law office together with Hayyut, another officer from the battalion. To this day Kugel visits Mintz's mother and was even at his brother's wedding. "Some-

times I don't understand how it can be that twenty
years have passed and there hasn't been a day that I
haven't thought about him" related Iris, the dead officer
Pundak's girlfriend. She was the last of the people I met
with, and when I spoke with her I felt that same choking lump in my throat that you sometimes feel in the
face of a sorrow that touches your soul. Her brother fell
in the Six Day War, and when she received no word
from Uri, who had been her beloved since fourth grade,
she was very anxious. It was on the war's second Saturday that a girl came to her house, bearing a letter that
Iris had written and which had been found in the pocket
of the officer who had been scorched by a phosphorus
shell and who was brought to Ichilov Hospital in Tel Aviv
unconscious and without any identifying marks. Pundak lay in the ward for a whole day, just a few hundred
yards from the homes of his girlfriend and his parents,
listed as unknown. It was only after he died that his
identity was discovered and word was sent to his girlfriend. "From that moment my life stopped. Once, a for-
tune teller looked at my hand and asked me where I had
been between '73 and '76. For me those are years that
were rubbed out. From the day that Uri died I was with
his parents for three years. I went with them to Copen-
hagen, and wherever else they went. They saved me and
even introduced me to the man I married a few years
after the war, in a wedding with ten people, no invita-
tions. My new husband was right for me because he was
a tank officer like Uri, tormented by the war and the loss
of his adopted brother, who had been killed. For years

my husband was the phantom while Uri was real, and I don't know how he put up with that sort of life. Only when my first son was born did I discover that I still had the ability to love, which I thought had been lost forever, and I didn't call my son Uri, because Uri is Uri and there is no other."

THE MAN WHO
DECIDED TO DIE

THE AIR FORCE AIR CONTROLLER dispatched Lanir into the Syrian missile death zone. By that time, on the eighth day of the Yom Kippur War, the Israeli Air Force was in smithereens, broken up into squadrons, each fighting for its life. Everyone realized that there was no one to trust up above, in the command, where the generals were screaming at each other and sending men against missile batteries without knowing how to get away from them. Up until then, the pilot Lanir's life had been something of a miracle. He'd bailed out and almost been killed and flown clean through a cloud of shrapnel from an exploding plane so many times. Even his father, a retired senior officer who'd pushed him hard to succeed, concluded that his son had better go into civilian life. But Lanir remained a soldier, to the end.

The first time he was almost killed was when he was in the backseat during a night flight in a training plane, a Fouga Magister. A Voiture pilot veered too close to Lanir's Fouga and snapped off its nose. Lanir saw the trainee in the front seat go deathly still, and then the plane plummeted like a stone. Lanir opened the canopy and ejected just in time, parachuting safely into a field. Three years later, he was tailing a Syrian MIG 21 and fired both his guns. The Syrian plane exploded so close in front of him that Lanir didn't have time to swerve away and flew straight into the fireball. The Mirage went black from the heat, the canopy was covered with soot, but Lanir got through it safely and landed under direction from the ground.

Two years later, during the War of Attrition, he descended on a convoy of Egyptian trucks near the Suez Canal. Firing his missiles, he dove so low that an exploding ammunition truck punched thousands of little holes in his plane. "It was a miracle," he told a friend of that near catastrophe. On another night during that war he only barely pulled out of a too-steep dive over an Egyptian vehicle. It seemed as if all his near misses were behind him when, two years later, as the commander of a squadron of Mirage 101s, Lanir's plane collided with another and went into a high-speed spin. Lanir bailed out. A commission of inquiry cleared Lanir of all responsibility in the matter, but he suffered an attack of guilt and considered resigning from the force. He was awfully hard on himself. Where others would have papered over a snafu, he put more pressure on himself. It took him a long time to get over it.

His parents wanted him to get out. He'd come too close to death too often, and they were afraid of the next time. Yet others urged him not to leave, and deep down he wanted to stay. "I never understood how close the game with death was," his widow told me many years later, "but I was afraid all the time. Nonstop fear. I developed a mechanism of knowing exactly when he was coming back. Not what he was doing, not where, only when he was coming back. I grasped at that in moments of panic. Around us, on the squadron base at Hatzor during the War of Attrition, friends were always getting killed, and some were taken prisoner. There I realized how it is that a madman willingly returns to the mental institution. It's because the people there are the ones you've been with through the worst."

During this time of clouds of fire and shrapnel, air battles and too-low dives, pilot Avi Lanir was already a solid young man with a definite view of the world, a very determined pilot and a pathological optimist, a man with a winning personal charm, a clear life plan, whom the air force expected great things of. He was among those few who had studied electronics engineering back in the 1960s and who were promoted into the air force leadership so as to leapfrog it into the 1970s.

As with anyone else, everything about Lanir could be traced back to the home he'd grown up in. He was born Avraham Lankin, during World War II, and when he was six months old, his father left home to join the Jewish Brigade in Europe in the war against the Germans. His father was absent for five years of Lanir's life. The mother and baby lived in a wooden hut in an orange grove in Herzliyya. The father was a tough, stern man, who cast a large shadow over his son. He was away from home a lot even after he returned from Europe, serving in the Israeli army, and then in the national security services. Though at home he was the focus of all adulation and respect, his father spoke little, and seldom warmly or in praise of his son. He instilled in his son a fierce desire to excel, making his life an unceasing struggle against failure and defeat. Those who were very close to Lanir would tell me that this need pulsed within him, perhaps until his end, in a lonely cell. There, alone with himself, he had to decide what he would do in the face of his Syrian interrogators, how to get the best of them. Perhaps he understood that death was preferable to speaking to his interrogators and returning home alive.

The relationship between Lanir and his lover, Michal, later his wife, also began as a kind of battle. If they both hadn't had easygoing dispositions, their love might have crashed and burned right at the start. It was a Romeo and Juliet story: she was of the house of the murdered man and he was of the house of the murderer. In 1960, Michal was novice pilot Lanir's instructor on a Link flight simulator. It took some time for things to heat up between them. On the first evening when they were alone on the beach at Ashkelon, Michal asked, "What party do you belong to?" Because she came from a very political, very left-wing home. Lanir was in shock at the question and didn't answer. When he remained silent, Michal asked: "What's the matter? Are you from the right?" "I'm not," he mumbled, "but they—not anymore," and so on.

When his girlfriend found out where exactly he came from, from what family and what background, an abyss opened up between them. It turned out that Lanir's uncle had been one of the commanders of the Etzel underground in Jerusalem—was, in fact, the man who decided on and carried out the assassination of Michal's uncle, a Jewish officer in the British-run police force. The uncle had been murdered in 1939, two years before she was born, and she grew up in her grandmother's house in the midst of constant weeping. The picture of the old woman's son, Uncle Arieh, hung on the wall, and under it the words "Murdered by Scoundrels." It was a sad house in which she imbibed with her mother's milk the belief that right-wing meant murderer. They had killed her uncle on a Jerusalem side street on suspicion of collaboration with the British. There on the beach Michal told the young pilot Lanir about the murder, and he was speechless. She kept their relationship secret from her grandparents, who died not knowing that Lanir was in fact a Lankin, sired by the pharaohs.

Enemies celebrated together at their wedding. The bride's people on the left, the groom's on the right. They matured, as if ignoring the past, but the death into which Michal had been born became an inseparable part of their lives—a constant companion even before the end came for Lanir. In '53, when she was a girl, her cousin, a pilot, had been killed in a crash; and in the Yom Kippur War, Michal's brother was killed in his tank. Her cousin Arik, who was named after the murdered uncle, was also killed, while serving as a maintenance officer in the paratroop corps. "Had my husband

---

not died, my grief for my little brother would have overcome me completely. He was like my own child. But twenty years went by before I could mourn him. It was only two years ago that I went to his grave for the first time. I have taken care not to live a life of mourning, because mourning frees you of all responsibility—like an addiction. The mourner expropriates the dead person from all others and takes sole possession of him. Houses turn into cemeteries. During these twenty-two years since the war I have often gone to console other mourners, and I've found that there are only two consolations: one, that the dead person didn't suffer—and the second consolation is that the children remember. And here is where my mysticism begins: that a person lives as long as people remember him. So, for me, personally, cemeteries are not important, but I take stories very seriously. When I dream about Avi, he isn't Avi at thirty but a man who has matured with me, who is my age today."

When you look at Lanir's eldest son, who was less than seven when his father fell into Syrian hands, you get a picture of what happened there on the air force base during the years before the war. A child is the most sensitive seismograph there is. In the tensest moments, he discerns, as children always do, what the adults want to keep hidden. From his very beginning, Lanir's son lived on the razor's edge and was the air base's wild child. He grew up during the War of Attrition, when every week a father in one of the homes around them was killed or taken prisoner. The fathers kept getting fewer, and Noam Lanir felt an urgent need to save his dad. At the age of five he climbed into a Mirage that was in a standby position and fired its landing parachute. Another time he fasted for a long period so that he'd shrink and get smaller and turn back time, take the family back to Haifa. In the midst of the huge noise of take-offs and scrambles—and the whispered tidings of Job— he had grown up at home with two adopted sisters, the two small daughters of a friend of his father's who was a POW in Egypt.

For the boy, his father was not just the commander of all the other children's fathers but also the source of his identity and social status. He could sabotage and tear apart half the base and still be petted and spoiled by the mechanics and secretaries. Every week he sat on his father's lap and took off into the skies in a light aircraft. When they flew to visit Grandma near Haifa, father and son would float along Mount Carmel and then suddenly dive into the plain. He always needed a huge amount of excitement, and his father felt a need to provide it to the limit. When a little girl was born, so like her father with her winning smile, father and son remained very close. He has many memories of just the two of them—like sitting in the Cessna as his father's hand guides him to the heights.

The war that came so suddenly, and the army's help-lessness when it began, were a heavy blow. Noam took his anger out on another kid and smashed his face in. At the time, they had been transferred, with all the other families, to the Ne'urim facility. Only the pilots and crews remained at Hatzor. In this new place, troubled Noam grew even wilder than before. The air force psychologist arrived to calm him down, telling him: Do you know why your dad isn't shooting down MIGs? It's because you're making trouble for your mom. Noam calmed down at once. He felt that a huge responsibility lay on his tiny shoulders. The next day Lanir shot down a MIG, and a day later his own plane crashed. Go tell a kid that there's no connection. He also remembers the secrets. Once he told his grandma on the telephone that new missiles had arrived and the line was cut off immediately. Another time Lanir took the boy to watch the secret trial flight of the prototype of the Kfir, which was called the Technolog. Because of his professional training, Lanir was one of the test pilots. It was a secret matter, and Noam remembers how they took the plane out of its hangar, how his father took off and landed, and how they threw buckets of water on him to celebrate the success.

He lived for many years with his childhood memories, until, as an adult, he began to look into his father's end. When he made inquiries, Noam learned that his father had not only been the Technolog's test pilot but had also belonged to the select air force team that had been assigned a special top-secret mission. It may well be that his inquiry was a way of mitigating the pain of loss, of giving meaning to the death that had taken his father from him at an age when he so needed him. "I can actually remember feeling horrible shame when I heard that my father had been taken prisoner, because that is the antithesis of hitting the enemy. Falling prisoner is defeat. In disappointment I said, 'Then he's a shitty pilot.' And another pilot yelled at me, 'Don't talk that way about your father.'"

The last time Michal and her husband saw each other was the evening before his fall. "We organized a bus to take the women who'd been evacuated from the Hatzor base to visit their husbands. The boy wanted to come and see his father, and I didn't want to take him even though Avi begged to see him. I arrived at our house in Hatzor and it wasn't a home. It had become a barracks full of pilots who'd been brought into the squadron. Avi, who was so modest that he gave our bed to another man, slept on Noam's child-size bed. Everything was very tense, the situation was horrible. 'You don't have to worry about me,' Avi said, 'but your brother Srulik is in a terrible place.'" Most likely he'd flown over the Vale of Tears and had seen from the sky the desperate battle below. Michal felt like someone who was walking a very narrow emotional rope, above an abyss.

"The house was filthy and I tried to clean. I spoke and was angry, and I remember every stupid detail of that visit that I knew would shake me emotionally. That was the last time I saw him. At midnight they rounded up all the girls. Everyone was in a good mood. Only I was depressed. At night, at midnight, I went over to my girlfriend Esther Eini and told her I was really terrified. I truly felt a catastrophe coming. The next day I drove to Kfar Shmaryahu and phoned the squadron. The secretary told me that Avi was busy and that he would call back as soon as he was free. A half-hour later I called again, because he hadn't called, and the secretary said that she had forgotten to tell him and that he'd already gone out on a flight. I screamed like a crazy woman and she said to me, 'What's your problem! In forty minutes, after the mission, he'll be landing and he'll call.' An hour later I called and someone I didn't know told me that Avi was still in the air. I hung up and knew: we're waiting for the messenger, something horrible has happened. It took less than an hour before they informed me that he'd fallen prisoner and that they'd seen two jeeps collect him, alive and well. I was optimistic for a few days, but then that passed. I have no idea why, but at some point I stopped believing. Not knowing is the most horrible thing. I think of all the families that wait for nine or thirteen years for news. Imagination knows no bounds.

"When they say 'killed,' it's a sharp knife. "Missing" is a dull knife. You can't live the whole time in a hell of imagination about how the son or husband is being tortured, alone in the dark, so a pendulum of despair and hope starts swinging—and that is a horrible situation, too. Nosiness is the dark side of Israeli vitality. They won't let you die in the street, but they'll get into your veins."

Four months went by from the time Lanir was taken prisoner until Secretary of State Henry Kissinger brought his lists. Kissinger was then soaring over the region like an airborne messiah. Michal refused to take part in the delegations of the families of Israeli MIAs who were organizing a trip to the United States to exert pressure. "On the day the lists arrived I was so afraid of the cold prophecies of my heart that I took sleeping pills and slept most of the time. At the end of that day I already knew that Avi wasn't on the list, that that was the end." His parents continued to believe, until the body arrived, in June. Then they broke. "A rabbi came to ask me questions that would make it easier to identify the body. When he left, he said, 'I'm sorry if I've hurt you.' I told him that when your entire body is a wound, what's another pinprick. No one came to reassure me that the body hadn't been tortured. Someone began to tell me that he'd sat with the pathologist and heard details, and I asked him to be quiet. I didn't want to know. I don't need any additional details for my imagination."

Midway through the eighth day, after a week of war of a type hitherto unknown, Avi Lanir and his number two, Yehoshua Shlan, were dispatched in two Mirages against Syrian MIGs in the Syrian central sector. A region teeming with missile batteries. Years later, Koren, the commander of the northern Mirage squadron, would say that he felt angry about what had happened to Lanir, because he could have refused the controller's instructions and not gone into an area teeming with missiles. There were new instructions issued, after a sortie the previous day, not to go into areas in which there were missile ambushes, but Lanir had not been present at the meeting at which that was decided on. The air controller directed them to the target. To the west of the Damascus road Lanir saw an explosion on the ground, and turned to locate an enemy plane. They were at an altitude of 12,000 feet when a Syrian SA missile rose from a ground battery and broke through the clouds.

Shlan saw the missile from his plane and shouted, too late, to break formation. The missile hit Lanir's Mirage. Below, on the ground, the men of Regiment 9 saw a plane falling and a parachute rocking not far from Dir al-Adas. Shlan, fleeing west from the missiles, also saw Lanir's parachute ejecting from the disintegrating plane.

The Israelis who watched the parachute's descent from their armored vehicles felt helpless. It was deep inside Syrian territory. There was no time to organize an effective rescue mission. Years later, the son, Noam, would find out that an order had been given to maintain a rapid rescue force, but was not carried out. Neither was a helicopter force sent. The curiosity that was roused many years after the war, especially on the son's part, would lead to several allegations—some of which cannot be adequately checked today. Go discover today what the correct version is, what really happened there. Other members of the family had no desire for an inquiry, an intrusion. Quite the opposite, they avoided intrusion. "I didn't want to open the stitches," Michal Lanir told me. "What good will it do now? I don't want them to investigate and find out that someone maybe made a wrong call and didn't send helicopters. After twenty-two years, picking through it is disgusting to me and I won't take part in it."

The observers on the ground saw that the jeeps quickly reached Lanir and concluded that his condition was okay. A while later a Syrian commando team was captured elsewhere, and one of its members said in his interrogation that he had been where Lanir fell and had seen officers dealing with him, not farmers or regular troops, who often vent their wrath on prisoners who fall into their hands. The Syrian related that Lanir, who emerged from cover behind some boulders, spoke French with them. He was, in that case, calculatingly concealing his excellent English. He knew that he was in their hands, perceived what was in store for him, and planned out, in detail, what he would do. It was his nature to make a decision and stand by it to the end.

The pilot Rokach, who abandoned his plane over Damascus, lay seriously wounded in the same hospital as Lanir. The Syrians had performed a lung operation on him, and a nurse kept watch over him to keep him from swallowing blood clots and choking. She saved Rokach, because he'd decided to die. Half conscious, in a morphine haze, Rokach heard a voice speaking to him from behind the curtain that hid the next bed over. Lanir gave him his full name and even spelled it out. He said that he was wounded in his arms and legs and was asking for morphine. "I got it real bad," he said, and sighed. Rokach remembered that the Syrian nurse made a sign to the effect that Lanir was done for.

Neither Rokach nor any other Israeli prisoner saw Lanir after that. He was hidden behind his curtain and afterwards returned to his solitary cell. In 1973 there was still the tradition of silence—the stories of Jibli who had not said a word in his Jordanian captivity, and of Uri Ilan, who had not betrayed his country as a POW in Syria. A man who fell prisoner felt as if his buddies' lives were in his hands, and that his suffering was the only thing that stood between him and betrayal. "I'm convinced that Lanir shut himself up, decided not to talk," a childhood friend told me about him. "Certain human beings can make a decision to remain silent. Avi was like that. Maybe he had an optimistic faith that he would be silent and still return alive. Maybe out of his faith in humanity, or in his interrogators, he concluded that if you were caught alive, you'd return alive." His son, Noam, gave me what seems to be the family version: "Dad was crazy stubborn. He kept silent and slipped away."

In the Syrian prison, the pilots understood that Lanir was with them somewhere. When the isolation period ended and they were together, the pilots would pronounce his name out loud each time the jailers entered their room. There was one male Syrian nurse who fled from the room each time they said Lanir, as if he knew something that was hard for him to bear. Maybe he saw him at the end. Lanir came home in early June. The body that had been returned was examined and found to have been tortured. Michal asked to meet with his number two, Yehoshua Shlan, who'd seen him last—but Yehoshua never came to her house. "Since then I've never asked to meet anyone, nor did I speak with Rokach. I made a rule for myself not to go into it. I kept myself in line. For twenty years I didn't read the Yom Kippur newspapers, with their accounts of the war, and I didn't read the report of the commission of inquiry on the war. To this day, my 'POW box' is closed. I locked it and threw away the key. It's an entirely exposed nerve. The thought about the loneliness and the pain of a man who is in the hands of people who want to make him hurt. Once I read an article about different forms of heroism, and the supreme one was withstanding solitude and not breaking. It mentioned Avi. Alone in your cell, you have no audience, you are already beyond humanity. To yourself, that is the greatest truth. I don't believe that anyone intended to kill him. They were the enemy and it was a war. I don't have anyone to hate."

Lanir was decorated for heroism posthumously. "The late Lt. Col. Avraham Lanir," the award said, "was tortured to death by his interrogators and revealed no information." Whoever wrote that must certainly have known the things that remained unsaid, that did not come out despite the agony. Two months after his funeral at the Mount Herzl Military Cemetery, Michal and her children left Hatzor and moved to a small city, to a neighborhood built for pilots' families. Noam threw stones at the windows of the new house, which had a peaceful view, uninterrupted by the thunder of warplanes scrambling above. Michal never married again. She taught school, earned her master's degree, and single-handedly brought up Noam and Nurit, whose smile was like her father's. "I built a home from ruins, held jobs, began a doctorate—and Avi grew with us all the time. Friends will tell you that I am an active woman. But it was only two years ago that I woke up suddenly, and it seemed to me that for twenty years I had been frozen, that life had run away."

WHOEVER KNEW
SHUT UP OR DIED

IT WAS ONLY WHEN ALIZA was in her fourth month of pregnancy that she remembered the family's lost baby—how when he was six months old the family had left him in the hands of a Polish woman, never to see him again. That tiny baby, laid out on an upholstered cushion, living in a world in which children were thrown into furnaces like tinder. The Polish woman took him, and after that the world turned over. There was a roundup, people disappeared, and then came the deluge, after which nothing remained as it had been. Anyone from the family who happened to remain alive looked out for himself, rose from the ruins, put himself back on his feet, moved to Israel. And here, in 1962, during her first pregnancy in Tel Aviv, while a baby was growing inside her, Aunt Aliza remembered the lost infant, and could not bear the thought that he'd been forgotten. So she began to ask around: Where was the boy who had disappeared without a trace? Thirty more years had to pass. It was only in 1994 that the family felt, for the first time, that the mystery of the lost baby might indeed be coming close to resolution.

The entire family asked itself whether the pink-faced man who descended from the Warsaw–Tel Aviv flight that Thursday was the lost baby. He was a Polish psychologist with blue eyes, born on exactly the same day as the baby, and he knew nothing about his past. I was also there when his plane arrived. Ilana and Yossi, who could be his brother and sister, and Aunt Aliza, who for years led the campaign to find the baby, waited in the arrival hall. Each with his own reaction. Ilana held a photograph of the man and trembled. Poles approached the passport control counters, drew out their documents, and here I saw a man with a light mustache, a bit confused and panicky, passing through the checkpoint, then stopping before Ilana. He bent slightly into the position of a Polish bow and kissed the hand of his lost sister, or of a total stranger.

The Kormans were a wealthy family with a leather-tanning business in the Polish city of Radom. They had a factory with huge vats in which animal skins were soaked in an astringent substance that removed the hair and left the skin entirely smooth. They lived in a large private house situated at the intersection of two fine streets, with a garden and an entranceway for wagons. Their grandfather had a synagogue of his own. In '42, at the height of the extermination, they were already far from their home. They had been transferred and shut up with many other Jews in the Radom Ghetto. The grandfather of the family, David, was detained by the Germans and severely beaten, and he died in agony after he was returned. The factory was still operating then, being vital for the German war effort. Luck and money kept the Kormans alive. They had four daughters and a son, Yossi. The mother, Hela, was in her final month of pregnancy. She had refused to abort the pregnancy despite the terror all around, because they so much wanted a son to be born to take the name of the dead grandfather. On June 11, 1942, the baby was born, at home, because of the danger—the impossibility, really—of going to the hospital. And it was decided, so that he might survive, not to circumcise him.

They gave him his name—David—in a small ceremony at home, with drinks. He cried, laid out on a white baby cushion with a commotion around him. Hersh, his father, decided, in consultation with his wife, Hela, that the baby would need to be protected in the event that they were sent to a labor camp. They had a very loyal factory guard, and they went to his wife, Mrs. Malczkowska, and asked her to find a Polish woman with whom the baby could be deposited. She brought a Polish woman to their home in the ghetto, and at their second meeting little David was already handed over to her. Aliza, the father's sister, remembers the moment of parting in the ghetto apartment, and how Hela had cried bitterly at being separated from her son. They

gave the woman money and baby clothes and all his nec-
essaries, and concluded an oral contract according to
which she would bring him to the factory twice a week
to show him to them as long as they were there. When
they returned from the camps, she would give him back.
When evening came, the Polish woman went off with
the baby, and Hela Korman was still weeping bitterly.

Before she went, the father brought a skin-dissolving
substance from the factory and made a small welt
on the baby's back, so that he could be identified when
the day came. Aliza, who was a young girl at the time,
remembers the burn, and how it was all done in secret,
and how they decided that only Hersh's sister, Rosa,
would know the Polish woman's address and would
make contact with her, if the others couldn't. A Polish
journalist who looked into the story years later said that
nowhere else had he encountered such precise planning
of a baby's rescue. But life can frustrate even parents'
best-laid schemes. Twice the Polish woman was able to
bring the baby to the factory and show them that he was
alive and healthy, and then there was a big round-up of
thirty thousand people, who were gathered together in
Radom on a huge lot under the command of drunken
Germans. No one was paying attention anymore to who
was rich and who was poor, or who had a work permit or
a certificate designating them an essential worker. Everyone stood in a long line, and a German gestured left
or right—who went on the train to Treblinka and who
remained. Hersh Korman, the father, was sent to the
train. His wife, Hela, was to stay behind, as were Yossi

and Ilana and Aunt Aliza and the girls. When just the remnants, those who were to remain, were still on a small part of the lot, Hela went up to a German and said that she wanted to stay with her husband. The German told her: You're a good-looking woman. Why do you want to die? They're not coming back.

He was drunk, and as she smelled his breath she began to run in the direction in which the thousands were going to the train, and the three girls ran after her. In the huge commotion, Aliza would never know if Hela and her daughters, running among the people, ever found her husband, or if the family was united in that last train ride. Aunt Aliza, together with Yossi and Ilana, returned to the little ghetto that was now just two streets. They spoke about the baby, but they could no longer go out, even to the factory. That's how contact was lost. In the next years, Aliza, who was a young girl, Ilana, who was twelve, and Yossi, who was ten, would go through all the tribulations and horrors of the Holocaust. When the war ended, Aliza's sister went to the guard's wife and asked her what had happened to the baby. Aunt Rosa was already dead, and no one knew where the Polish woman lived. The guard's wife responded testily: "He got sick, and she handed him over to a convent and later heard from someone that he died there." That's all she said.

Her husband, the factory guard, remained faithful to the family. At the end of the war he revealed to the same sister who'd come to him the location of a treasure the father of the family had hidden in the factory yard.

The family did indeed find it and divided it up among each so they could begin a new life in the postwar world. In 1975, in a new Poland awash in hatred and in guilt over its collaboration with the Nazis, the faithful guard put an end to his life. The Korman family, who knew how loyal he had been, suspected that the baby's fate may have had something to do with his suicide— perhaps he knew that his wife had not been honest with them. Aliza says that the family was divided, between the men and the women, about looking for the baby. The women searched unceasingly and in every way; the men were skeptical and demanded proof in black and white. "I feel like a mother who is searching for her child. I have to give an accounting to his dead parents, to my brother. I need to feel I did everything possible to find him," Aliza told me, speaking of her desire to protect that baby who, if he was still alive, would be a man of about fifty.

In 1962, during her first pregnancy, Aliza began to think about what she would have done had she been in a similar situation and had to give up her baby in order to save it. The surviving daughter, Ilana, the baby's sister, was also pregnant then, and the two women took counsel. After their babies were born, the need to find out grew stronger, and they began to correspond with the guard's wife, the same Malczkowska who was living secure in Communist Poland. Her only reply was: "If you want your furniture and your piano, I am willing to return it all. But about the boy and the Polish woman who took him, I have nothing more to say."

Stymied in the face of this silence, they turned for

help to the Israeli authorities. A woman from the security services was sent to Radom and spoke with Malczkowska, but she would not tell the agent the Polish woman's name, nor where she lived. Communist Poland refused to grant the Kormans a visa, and it was not until 1983 that they finally reached Radom, only to find that the guard's wife had died two years earlier. So they missed the last woman who knew where the baby had gone. But there was still the guard's wife's daughter. She had been a ten-year-old girl during the war and surely would have heard conversations at home. She would certainly know, they reasoned, who the Polish woman was. They went to her house, but she refused to talk. When her husband, a senior government official, came home, she asked them to go. A year later they appealed, on a Polish television and radio program, to the public for help. Warm responses arrived from people who wanted to help, but no hint of the Polish woman's identity turned up. A family friend in Poland named Papocz represented them in the searches there. A man of about forty came to him, claiming that he was the lost baby. He showed some marks on his abdomen, but it was soon determined that he was someone else.

It was only in 1994, after a rebroadcast of the show about their search, that a Polish psychologist from Cracow, a man by the name of Wicek Soborski, contacted Papocz and asked how he could contact the family. Because he was the lost baby of the Jews, born on precisely the day the little child Korman had been born. He also had a mark on his skin.

From the time of his childhood as an orphan, Soborski remembered that each night he had dreamed of a
man with a black beard who came to take him, and he
didn't know why. He grew up in a German orphanage in
Poland, and at the end of the war Polish nuns of the
Order of St. Joseph came and took him. When he was
six years old—up to that age he remembers nothing,
except one good friend—the nuns handed him over to a
woman who was sixty-one years old, a childless teacher
who wanted a little boy. Her name was Florentina So-
borska, and her husband, seventeen years younger than
she, was named Marion. Children chased after Wicek in
his new neighborhood and called him a foundling. He
was miserable in the home of the elderly teacher, and
when he grew up he quickly got married in order to set
up a home for himself.

At the age of twenty-five, when he already had a little girl of his own, he began to search out his past. The
orphanage had closed and become a medical testing
facility, and no documents remained there. He located
Sister Celestina, who remembered him as a war orphan.
She was ninety-one by then, but entirely sound of mind;
she even remembered how she had baptized him herself
and given him the name Wicek, because the German
woman had called him Walter. You were a war orphan,
she told him, but she didn't know anything about his
origins. The only thing written on his certificate was
the exact date of his birth, the same day in June, 1942,
that the little Korman baby had been born. That was all
that Wicek Soborski had from his early past—the day

he came into the world. The teacher who had adopted him died in 1972, and his adopted father died four years before he landed in Tel Aviv. He looked through their papers and found a letter the teacher had sent to her husband, who was in Warsaw at that time, in '48. There she described how she had gone to the orphanage and taken away a boy of six, and how happy the boy was, and how he held out his hands to her because he wanted a mother. The adoption was carried out without documents, in the midst of the postwar chaos, when a sixty-one-year-old woman could show up and simply take an orphan boy for herself. But the letter clearly included the words "Jewish orphan."

From that moment, Wicek, who was a Catholic by training, understood that he was a Jew. Until that day he had lived with his wife and children as a nonpracticing Catholic. All those years his friends had known that he was an orphan who envied them their families and their pasts, and when they heard the program on the Kormans they told him. So Aunt Aliza received a thick letter from Poland—"and when I opened it in the post office, I felt I was dying on the spot, because seven photographs fell out of it, of a small boy, a teenager, and a man, pictures of Wicek, who might be David Korman." The family quickly decided to bring him to Israel for a tissue compatibility test that would determine if he was the lost brother.

Flight 455 from Warsaw landed half an hour early, and Ilana was standing there with her daughter, who recorded the entire story on a home video camera.

While they waited, holding Wicek's photographs, a man with a bristly yellow mustache came over and took Ilana's hand to kiss it. She looked completely frozen, quiet, keeping all the storm inside her. Ilana's conversation with Soborski was casual, like a white ripple on waters churning deep down. They went to stand by the baggage-claim carousel. They spoke in Polish about this and that, how the flight had been, how it had left Warsaw at nine in the morning, and how things were in Poland. Hard, hard, and there's never enough money for anything. Soborski was wearing a gray sports jacket and held a light piece of hand luggage. When his suitcase arrived we saw it was a very light cloth bag. Dana, a daughter, surveyed him with X-ray eyes. He has the family's hands, she said. But he looks very different from the Kormans, who are all dark and broad-faced. "No, there was one fair sister, who was murdered."

The fifty-year-old orphan stood tense and erect. For the first time in his life he was in an unfamiliar "capitalist country," as he put it. He was surrounded by the watchful eyes of people who were either his siblings or utter strangers. A moment before they drove to Ilana's house in Tel Aviv—a nice home, surrounded by greenery—they stood by the cars to have their picture taken. The airport's palm trees swayed above them in the warm Israeli breeze. Wicek hugged his sister and brother, or two strangers, and they looked together at the camera and drove away. On Saturday we sat with him at a fish restaurant facing the Jaffa beach, where brother Yossi took us, drawn by the sight of the water that stretched from here to the shores of Europe. A warm friendship was already beginning to develop with Wicek. "He's a nice, modest man," Yossi said of him, "and we'll be family anyway, no matter what the tests show."

Whether out of embarrassment, or out of a feeling that they had to trust him, they did not look at the welt that the father had given him in the ghetto apartment in Radom. Anyway, if he was a con man, he could have scarred himself, since no one knew exactly what it looked like and whether such a mark would remain on the soft skin of a baby. It was seven in the evening and Wicek looked at the sun, which was just sinking in the water, and said that he would like to be part of the family. The next day he went for the test and remained a few more days with the brothers and sisters. Two weeks passed before the negative results arrived, and the sad conundrum of the lost baby returned to its starting point in 1942. Wicek the fifty-year-old orphan also cried a great deal, as he told them in a long, aching letter from Poland.

ON THE EDGE

WE TALKED ABOUT KLEISY ROBINSON in the dark of the car the whole 120 miles back to Tel Aviv. About what had happened there that night in her last moments on the cliff, where mountain goats search for water when darkness falls. What made her jump from the rocky ledge? The question doesn't let you go, even after you hear the whole story. And neither her husband, nor her small children, nor her friends have a complete answer. The same holds for the letter she left behind, two pages of Portuguese, which her husband reads again and again and does not comprehend. What I write will also be but an attempt to collect slivers from people who were around, and to take a look at the place where it happened, a small town, in the midst of the desert, on a crater's edge.

You're into the desert right after Beersheba. A narrow road stretches between rock-strewn hills. In the late morning it is still chilly. We passed by a few army tent camps. Smoke rose from shower chimneys, a Bedouin crossed the road with his herd of sheep, a clump of trees stood in a puddle of water that had collected around their roots. Fifty miles from Beersheba, at the entrance to Mitzpeh Ramon, next to a bus stop made of thick concrete, we saw four Russian immigrants amusing themselves with a newborn puppy. Bubki, Bubki, they called him, petting his head, as if consoling themselves for the desert that suddenly surrounded them. They sought warmth of a different kind in his fur, speaking a babbly Russian as if to a baby. Silence prevailed in the little city. When I arrived, it was two weeks since the tragedy had occurred. Kleisy's body had lain in Tel Aviv for a week and had then been flown to Brazil, to the place where she'd been born, where her parents awaited their daughter's coffin. She was buried as she wished, not in the desert soil of Mitzpeh Ramon. Her father began his *shiva*, his seven days of mourning, only after the distant burial. A stone was placed on the grave in the Jewish cemetery of Porto Alegre, almost a full day's flight away.

Twenty-eight-year-old Kleisy (born Martinez), her husband, Arieh, and their three children were part of the small South American community in Mitzpeh Ramon. A group of about sixty people—Argentinians, Brazilians like the Robinsons, Uruguayans, and Colombians. Little by little, they came together in Mitzpeh Ramon in recent years. They had all come from somewhere else and now met once a week beside the charcoal smoke of the *asado*, with meat they prepared in the woods, or in the open, or on trips to Eilat, on birthdays and at weddings. Young people, and types who had had trouble being accepted elsewhere, or had gone through traumas of illness or the collapse of a business. Like the Robinsons' good neighbor, Mauricio, who was also the chairman of their organization in Mitzpeh Ramon. He's a stocky guy, happy and good-hearted, who took me from place to place so I could write this story. Mauricio arrived in this place after his carpentry business fell apart. After extricating himself from his troubles, he migrated southward, to the tranquility of Mitzpeh Ramon, where you could buy a home of your own with a little yard for a modest sum and, perhaps, make a new beginning. Everyone lived in townhouses built for the army when it withdrew from Sinai. The place had stood empty for a long time. The Robinsons also moved into one. Small rooms, two floors, attached houses. They went before an absorption committee that checks to make sure there is no criminal record, and they began a life in a new place, like a second immigration, with new friends, a new job, a new school, a new home, a new view from the window, bitter cold at night, and unfamiliar heat during the day.

In a birthday photograph, I saw Kleisy Robinson sitting close to her grandmother, who had moved to Israel at the age of sixty-two with her daughter and granddaughters. The grandmother's hand lies on her granddaughter's shoulder. Kleisy's broad face is meditative. She was close to Grandma Fuchs. They spoke Spanish together. A young girl and an old woman sitting under an old clock that had been brought from Argentina and had stopped running here. "And I don't know what to think," the old woman told me. "I ran into Kleisy a while ago. A young girl, not happy, I don't know what to think about what she did." So the old woman said in Spanish, with her granddaughter translating for me. All in all, a warm, pleasant Latin community that held off loneliness.

On Friday, a day before she jumped to her death, Arieh and Kleisy sat at home with their two sons and the baby girl. They were watching television, put the kids to sleep, and around midnight received a phone call from Brazil, from Arieh's family. Arieh spoke on the phone about how the Germans had sent arms and money to Israel and Kleisy shouted: "The money the Germans sent won't solve our problems at the bank!" The subject of their debt to the bank was a part of their lives, a trouble that weighed on them like a stone. But no one had any idea how deeply it affected Kleisy. After the phone call, Arieh went to sleep. Kleisy stayed in the little living room with the yellow linoleum floor to watch television until late. Then she went to sleep beside Arieh. It's quiet at night in Mitzpeh Ramon; there is no sound of passing cars, or people walking past the window. The houses on Ein Ofarim Street huddle together like frightened sheep in the wilderness. In the morning Arieh woke up to the sound of the baby crying. He went to little four-month-old Shira's bed to feed her. Kleisy continued to sleep deeply until two in the afternoon. The day before she had been upset and very tense, so Arieh let her sleep late. There was food for the weekend in the refrigerator. At two she woke up tranquilly, showered, put on gray corduroys, a jacket, and a winter coat over it. She took some paperbacks, a notebook, and a pen and said she was going over to visit some friends. It was about three-thirty when she left the house and the family she would never see again.

When night and darkness came, Kleisy had not come home. It was bitterly cold outside. Arieh fed the children and put the baby to bed. At eight-thirty there was an air-raid siren, which he ignored. The television reported that an Iraqi missile had fallen on the desolate E zone. He made a few phone calls to friends to ask if Kleisy was with them but did not find her. By eleven-thirty he was very worried. He checked the children's beds and saw they were all sleeping, then locked the door and went to look for her. He didn't go into the homes of any friends, just walked around the streets. The Robinsons had a discreet way of dealing with their problems. They had also concealed the severity of their economic plight. That may explain why Arieh asked no one's help, why he didn't mention his fears to anyone, why he didn't ask anyone to watch the children while he was gone.

He came home, alone, after midnight and drowsed on the living room couch. He fell asleep and didn't hear the siren at one-thirty A.M. The house was deep in a heavy slumber. At that time Kleisy was already lying broken on the rocky ledge, in the bitter cold of the desert night. When he woke up on the couch in the morning, the baby was still asleep. Arieh asked the children to calm Shira if she woke up and went—as it was already Sunday morning—to see whether Kleisy had arrived at the nursery school she ran. He walked around a bit. The nursery school was closed. "I didn't tell the police because I knew that they don't look for missing people until twenty-four hours have gone by." Again he made a few circuits of the town and this time told friends that she was missing—and a little past noon he told the police. At two-thirty on Sunday afternoon the nature reserve ranger was informed that a search was commencing. Later in the afternoon Arieh went to the police station to tell them that he was also going out to search. They wouldn't let him enter the station. Someone kept him at the door for half an hour. Go home, they told him, as if they already knew something. Go home, let us look for your wife. From his position at the door, he heard them mentioning the area in which she would later be found. Five more tense hours went by before the local rabbi, together with a friend and a policeman, came to his house to tell him she'd been found.

They had met in São Paulo eight years before her death. That's a giant Brazilian city with thirteen million inhabitants, noisy and full of troubles—like insane inflation, military rule, anarchy, life that became harder day by day. A land of want in the midst of beauty, immense wealth, and color. Kleisy Martinez was nineteen when they met. A pretty girl, with a full, smiling face, who came from giant Brazil's south, from a mountain town named São Borja, in a cold region along the Argentinian border. It was a developed region, inhabited by people of German and Italian descent. São Borja's people speak Portuguese with an accent unlike that of São Paulo, and live 900 miles away from the huge metropolis. Orchids bloomed at the roadside in the São Borja of her childhood, just as daisies bloom in Tel Aviv. The beauty of the place where she had lived until her parents divorced and she moved to São Paulo would remain etched in her memory in Mitzpeh Ramon. They lived together a year in São Paulo, but Kleisy pushed for them to move to Israel. Their first son had already been born, and she felt insecure in Brazil's mad inflation. In her romantic way, she dreamed of the new world awaiting them. So they picked themselves up and left Brazil. They no longer had any property to sell or jobs to leave. Only the desire to move from the commotion and profound uncertainty of Brazil to a place where they would feel security under their feet. They landed on a kibbutz, moved to another kibbutz, and in the end arrived at what they thought would be their safe haven—Mitzpeh Ramon. At the time, before the great Russian immigration, anyone who came to Mitzpeh was warmly received. The city was half-empty.

The first thing that caught the eye of Kleisy's search party was the book she had left at the edge of the cliff, under the notebook, on a jutting tooth of boulder, where she had sat before her death. It was the Portuguese translation of a book called *The Price of Honor*, and it's hard to think of a better name for the last part of her life. The book's cover shows a blond girl, as pretty as Kleisy in her youth. It's a modern legend in soap-opera style about a poor immigrant who got rich and won power and influence in his new land—all the fantasies that the Robinsons never realized. When does the fantasy of wealth cease to be a consolation and instead simply serve to highlight your own poverty? The Robinsons were immigrants who had had no luck. Unsophisticated, inexperienced, and young in an unfamiliar land, they bought a small home and furniture with a mortgage and built up a great amount of debt. The manager of the local bank was replaced. The one who had given everyone easy credit on good terms left. A new manager arrived with stricter orders. The Robinsons reached a settlement arrangement, but it didn't cover all their debts. Their cosigners received warnings and began to complain to the Robinsons. They felt increasing pressure, but their friends said don't worry, it will all work out. They were ashamed of their problems even with close friends. During the final week of Kleisy's life, a new couple arrived in Mitzpeh Ramon, friends of Kleisy's from Brazil. Rita, her good friend from São Paulo, her husband, and their small son. Rita, a pretty woman with hair pulled back and a small scar near her mouth, remembers that she also spoke with Kleisy about their debts—"but who doesn't have debts?" They spoke about the pressure of living far from their families in Brazil. The idea of death as an escape also arose in their discussions, but Kleisy said that she would never kill herself, because of the children.

"Now it is beginning to get dark and very cold, but I am not afraid," Kleisy said at the end of the two pages she left behind for her beloved Arieh. "I am sorry, and what most hurts me is the children." She wrote about the baby whose birth they had so anticipated, the debts, her anger, about the bank manager, about her wish not to be buried in Mitzpeh Ramon, and about how she wanted Arieh and the children to move from there back to Brazil.

I climbed the cliff with the ranger, to the spot where Kleisy had jumped. It was the hour when it began to get dark, somewhere after five-thirty, when the sun casts deep shadows over the crater. Soon mountain goats would thread the narrow paths to the nearby water hole. They would also pass the place where Kleisy had sat, on a ledge above the abyss. Here she left her notebook, paperback, and pen, and there, below, marking the location of her fall, one red shoe remained. She had left home at about three-thirty. She'd walked for more than an hour before reaching this place, which lies not far from the alpaca farm, the home of those lithe South American animals. When the Robinsons still had a car, they would, on nice days, drive out to the crater, or to the observatory. They'd stopped at the place where she'd jumped several times, and Kleisy had said that it had the most beautiful view of the crater. The view is indeed breathtaking. A huge silent lunar landscape, cliffs and drops, the observatory, a small grove of trees, and at the bottom a dry riverbed. Wolf and mountain goat and leopard trails sometimes cross here. She sat for a long while before she fell. Had she already made the decision to jump, or had she decided here, overlooking the wild wadis, to spread her wings and fly? Perhaps the darkness cast its loneliness over her, a loneliness in which all memories were swallowed up, and the voices of her children, too, and everything, everything was forgotten except the desire to put an end to her misery.

At four-thirty on Sunday afternoon, three parties specially trained in searching for missing people and cliff casualties went out to look for Kleisy. The search began, by coincidence, precisely at the place she'd jumped, the ranger recounted, "because here there's an excellent view of a huge area. I got here with my jeep and parked it, and here I immediately found the notebook and the paperback under it, and the pen under it rolled away. The impressions where she sat on the step. Here are the drag marks of the descending rappellers. I went down to see her. She lay on her back and her face was to the side, undamaged. She stopped on a pile of fallen stones. I immediately sent word, and two people rappelled down to her, and checked her according to the doctor's orders. Death was established." Then they called in an air force helicopter, and soldiers sent up flares, which rose and then descended, their yellow light shrouded under tiny parachutes. Because of the strong night wind the helicopter could not get her out. Only the civil guard could do that, at close to eight in the evening, despite the many difficulties. They knew that she couldn't be left there, a place where jackals and wolves roam, until morning.

Mauricio the neighbor was sent with his civil-guard rifle to accompany the body to the hospital in Beer-sheba. He returned alone to Mitzpeh Ramon. Three people went to Arieh to tell him. They told the children that their mother had gone to the crater and fallen. The two boys began to fight over their collection of colored marbles, and years would go by before they understood what had happened to her, and how far away she was buried, there in Porto Alegre, where the orchids poke out from the fertile land, without anyone looking after them.

THE KURD'S SEVEN BEDS

I MET ELIAHU, Efrayim Zaken's sixth son, when I was on reserve duty in a dusty army pharmaceutical warehouse. The soldiers, American volunteers and Israeli reservists, assembled at a small medical corps base to sort through countless containers of expired pills and IVs, sterile needles and contaminated bandages. It was a strange group of people—the easygoing and the antlike, the short-tempered and the infinitely patient. There was a Yemenite guy named David Koresh, just like the leader of the cult that had been destroyed by fire; two quiet brain-injured veterans from past wars; an elderly American man who labored over short stories for a creative-writing workshop in Philadelphia; and a recently discharged soldier from the Galilee who dreamed of meeting a rock star. There was also a man from Jerusalem named Eliahu Zaken who was exempt from almost all duties. He was a short, muscular, thickset guy who looked as if he'd been packed into his skin by a compressor. He radiated tremendous physical strength, seeming always to be lying in wait for a victim to ignite his anger. He didn't go anywhere without his friend Tzfaniah, who was in appearance his exact opposite— tall and as thin as a starved man. Their friendship was of the type that is a soft, woolly mitten one moment and a clenched fist the next. It quickly became clear that both of them were Kurdish Jews, from the same neighborhood, and that they had the same exemptions from guard duty, from standing in the sun, from sleeping on the base, and from everything else. Each of them knew the other down to the very last detail of their families.

"You'll never see a Kurd with glasses, you'll never see a Kurd divorced, you'll never see a Kurd with an earring on his ear," said Zaken, ticking off the strict code of his community. During lunch break, when we sat a while under the eucalyptus tree by the mess hall, he spoke about missing Kurdistan and how they now travel there over forbidden borders and go to their homes in Iraq. From the first moment that we got into conversation, so vital to the soul in such a monotonous workplace, Zaken spoke warmly of his Kurdish compatriots, like a man who yearned for the tribe he had been born into even when he was away for but a day. He told of his wife, who obeyed his every order, and of the neighbors, who were wary of his anger. But when he mentioned his father, Efrayim, his face lit up. He spoke of the sweet tea mixed with ants that his ninety-two-year-old father drank in the middle of the night, of his seven beds, and of his journeys to the fishermen of Tiberias—just as someone else would recount, upon returning from a trek to the ends of Asia, the tale of an ancient mountain shepherd who lives in a cave.

The week my reserve duty ended I traveled to Jerusalem to meet Eliahu and his father. Efrayim Zaken's house lies on a narrow walkway in Katamonim, an old Jerusalem neighborhood that had once had a bad name because of its poverty and crime. But the area around Efrayim's house looks like a placid little village: stone-faced concrete houses built by the Jewish Agency forty years ago, stuck into a landscape of boulders and small gardens. The sense of poverty was mitigated by trees planted by the inhabitants. Efrayim's son pointed out, before we entered, the crawl space between the house and the ground, under the patio stairs. Inside were the iron trunks the family had brought from the city of Zaku when they came to Israel in 1950. Inside, still waiting, were eating utensils and black frying pans, stewpots and tin bowls, and a kerosene stove. Alongside them, in the darkness under the house, I saw a pile of firewood that the old man had chopped for the campfire he lights for himself in the winter.

In the little garden was a barrel of water that the municipal gardener filled for him so he could water his plants and wash his face. There were a few tobacco plants and watermelon vines, a young fig, a palm, and a plum tree, roses, and a pomegranate tree. "Everything my father plants grows for him and blooms and gives fruit like nowhere else." As I peeked under the steps, the old man emerged and invited me into the house. He was short and strong, like his son, and his years were not visible on his body. He swayed a bit as he walked, like a fishing boat, and his face was covered with bristles like a thistle field. His eyebrows were thick, his mustache clipped, and there was hair on his ears and stubble on his cheeks. The door was open, and the summer that lay over Katamonim pushed its way in and blended with the odor of tobacco and old things. We went into a room in which there were three unmade beds and a table with an open bowl of tobacco, a few old pieces of furniture hand-repaired, as on Robinson Crusoe's island, and other items, like a mattress and a woolen blanket, a chair and a cabinet, each of which had a history and a life of its own. Hanging on the wall was a scale that the old man had made from two flowerpots, a stick, and string, using an unopened package of sugar as its standard weight.

In an adjoining shaded room there were another three beds. An old couch rested on the front porch. "Each night he chooses himself a bed for the night, according to the heat," his son glossed for me. Since his six children had left home and gone to their families, the old man could choose whichever bed his heart set on, and he went from one to the other like a king among his wives. When it was very hot he slept on the bed outside, and wasn't scared. When his son raised the mattress to look for an old photograph, I saw a rusty ax and a hard wooden hoe handle for self-defense. When it wasn't as hot he went inside and slept by the open window. If it was a bit cool he slept in the corner bed, which had a board next to the wall to keep the chill out. When snow fell on Katamonim in the winter he slept in the inner room, which was entirely closed off, next to a kerosene heater. He slept lightly by habit, just as he had slept in Kurdistan next to the mule, on stones, with only his rucksack under his head. As his son explained about the seven beds, the father brought a bowl full of green figs bursting with sweetness that he had picked from a large tree he had received fifteen years ago as a tiny seedling from an Arab from Beit Safafa. "I made a hole in the ground and I put the tree in and I swore that I would never sell the figs but give them out to people so they could make a blessing on them in my wife's name," he related. The tobacco was also from his garden. He picked it and dried it in a large cloth sack and rolled himself cigarettes.

A dry wind came in through the door like a welcome guest, and the Jerusalem house suddenly looked to me like a village home that had been picked up from its place in Kurdistan by the Ararat Mountains during the great immigration of the 1950s and brought here on eagle's wings, complete with its floor and low ceiling, its small columns, its garden and rocky soil, its pomegranate and fig trees and tobacco plants. A cane hung on the cabinet—"in case my father gets old and needs it."

As we sat on the bed and talked, it turned out that Efrayim Zaken had been born in Kurdish Zaku in the third year of the twentieth century, when it was still part of the huge Turkish Empire. His father had been a clothing merchant there. They lived next to the river and he still has a memory, from the age of thirteen, or a bit more, of playing with some other boys by the river and suddenly seeing a plane in the sky that left a trail of smoke and sent them running in fear. That night not a Turk remained and the British came in. He remembers the Indian soldiers who came over the iron bridge that was right across from the family house on a tributary of the Tigris. The British demanded taxes on the vine-yards and insisted that they install toilets and other hygienic facilities. Up until then everyone had done their business in the river, where they also washed their clothes and bathed and drank. "They forced us to dig pits in our yards."

When the British left, the Iraqis remained, "and that was a good government," Efrayim said. He described how once, when thieves came to a house in the Jewish neighborhood and the master of the house and his wife caught them, the government hanged the thieves. A firm hand with burglars and the gallows for murderers are, for him, evidence of honesty and security. Efrayim grew up under Iraqi rule. He left his father's tutelage and himself became a merchant dealing in dry goods and wool. Most of the time he left his family at home in Zaku and went to the mountains to trade, climbing with his mules laden with goods across the Ararat Mountains. He knew the mountains, and the bandits as well. They came to his house and at times he slaughtered sheep for them and they ate together. They knew him and the route he always took, and once they lay in wait for him on the mountain when he rode there loaded with merchandise and money. He was with his little nephew, Jum'ah, who's now a cab driver in Jerusalem. The robbers ambushed him at a bend in the trail and captured the two of them. They tied him up, beat him up with a stick, but did not cut his throat, as they usually did, because he had hosted them in his house. "My mouth was stuffed with a handkerchief so I couldn't shout, and the boy told me that the bandits' guard had already gone. I got the handkerchief out and untied my hands with my teeth and sent Jum'ah to the Kurdish policeman so that he'd call for help. The boy went to the village and shouted: 'They killed Efrayim and took five mules with goods!' I could barely move because of the beating, and I was afraid the robbers would come back and take revenge. So I crawled inside a tree and the villagers came and shot a rifle and the bandits panicked on the mountain and left the mules and fled. A Kurdish doctor came and examined me, and he ordered a sheep slaughtered and took its skin with its blood and put a dressing and his medicines on the skin and wrapped me in it and made it very tight. I slept all that night in the warmth of the fur, and in the morning I woke up fresh like a baby."

To this day he has respect only for the old doctors, for herbal remedies and bloody furs that warm bruises. He's got only contempt for modern doctors who take money and give little pills that only hurt you. When, a few years ago, he got mixed up at night and instead of drinking from the juice bottle in the refrigerator drank a bottle of bleach, he saved himself by drinking milk and juices and water and sent away the ambulance that the neighbors had called, because they thought he was going to die. A few times, his son Eli told me, his father had chased and struck him when he saw his son brushing his teeth with toothpaste or washing his face with soap, which are things that hurt people and bring only problems. To this day, when he gets a bone-deep cut, Efrayim puts urine or arak on it and afterwards wraps the wound in tobacco and everything heals. And go tell him that at the age of ninety-two he has to start going to the doctor, when honey, garlic, and butter heated in a frying pan cure him overnight of the worst things that happen in his stomach.

When he was about fifty, and had six children—little Eli was a year old then, and Yosef, the baby, hadn't yet been born—Efrayim left all his property, homes and vineyards, sheep and horses, in Zaku. He took a few things, like a suitcase full of household items and gold. He signed a declaration to Iraq, according to which he was giving up everything and would never set foot there again, and came to young Israel, to an immigrant tent camp. There he raised goats and donkeys, and from there he moved to the neighborhood built for them on the hill slope in Katamonim. For thirty-seven years he worked as a construction worker and raised his children, and his wife worked at home, until she died, twenty years ago, of complications from a kidney condition, and all that remained was her photograph on the wall as a young woman, and her thin white scarf in the cabinet.

"As long as Mother lived it was a normal home, and when she went," her son Eli told me, "Father became free, alone, without anyone to tell him what to do. He decided when to do laundry, did only what was convenient for him. Within a short time he reverted to the old time and lived like there, in Zaku. He enjoys everything, arranges everything for himself. He bought himself an old scale, a meat grinder, doesn't change clothes, doesn't buy new ones, works in the garden all the time. Or he goes to the old Kurds' club and plays dominoes, pleased as punch with life. He cooks himself good food whenever he wants." Where other old men retreat into loneliness and longing for the dead, Efrayim went back to living his old Zaku life, with the harmony of one who works the land.

The outside door was made of iron. Next to it was a broken broom that had been rejoined, tables handmade out of boards, and beds resting on cinder blocks. The new wing of the house, with its new purple tiles, shiny bathtub, and modern kitchen, stood abandoned. The old man set up the tiny old kitchen for himself, with its one wooden ledge, on which were old, finely honed knife blades wrapped with rope so they could be handled. There were also old oiled pans, an old-fashioned refrigerator crammed with meat, a single-flame gas stove. Everything was wrapped in age, not clean and not filthy. His wife's death and his life alone allowed him to shed all that was new.

Brown ants ate the sugar in the open bowl in the kitchen, and when the old man scooped two spoonfuls into his tea at night, the insects got scooped up with it. I saw a moth that had climbed into and drowned in the open half-bottle of arak in the cupboard. "There's a moth in your arak," I told him. "What harm will it do me," Efrayim laughed. Field mice sometimes crossed the room as if they owned the house, and a snake slithered through the door that was always left open in the summer. A while ago, the old man and his son set an ambush for the snake, which had struck fear in the hearts of the family who lived on the second floor. At two at night, as Efrayim and Eli sat in wait under the fig tree, they heard a rustle and killed the snake with a hoe. The next day they hung him on the tree so the rest of the snakes would see it and quake.

Efrayim, in his old age, did not recall his past with longing. He simply lived happily. As we spoke he suddenly broke forth in song. He sang, as if he were addicted to happiness, about Abdul Hamid, who had gone to battle and fought his cousin. His fingernails drummed on the table as he recounted the tribulations of the war of the Kurds, in their old language. Afterwards he went out into the yard with the photographer, and I laid my head down peacefully on the unmade couch and drowsed to the comforting tick-tock of the wall clock that the son wound once every two weeks. Enveloped in the aroma of tobacco, I rested under strings of dried okra and peppers and little bags of seeds. Eli, the son, told me that whenever he needs a break from his home and his family he comes to his father's house, puts his head down on one of the seven beds, and falls right to sleep. His best friends also come sometimes, chat a bit with the father, put down their heads, and sleep. They get up two hours later, wash their faces, and leave the pleasant accommodations, or stay and listen to Efrayim sing in the evening about Abdul Hamid after a glass of the arak with the moth. He's still got a wanderlust from his merchant days in the Ararat Mountains. Even when he was a builder, he worked all over the country, and since he stopped working he goes on traveling. He goes to the Arabs in Bab al-Amud to buy things, or to Hebron, where he looks just like a Palestinian elder. He talks politics with them and doesn't trust them. Even though he fears no man or animal, he is afraid of the day when the Arabs will rise up against the country and destroy it.

Twice a week he goes down to the Ha-Tikva market in Tel Aviv to buy a cow's head or a large fish head, which he brings home to cook up with vegetables for himself and his sons. He has a sharp hunting knife with which he minces the flesh finely, stuffing tomatoes and peppers with it. Then he puts a heavy brick on the pot cover so that everything will be under pressure and cook just right. Once a week Efrayim takes the seven A.M. bus from Jerusalem to Tiberias. He gets there at ten and walks—this is a strong ninety-two-year-old man—from the bus station to Techelet Beach, to the fishermen's harbor, just as they are returning with their boats. They sell him six or seven pounds of small and large fish from their catch, at half price, and he puts them in his old plastic basket and goes for a short swim in the Sea of Galilee. Afterwards, he moistens the towel he has brought with him, wraps the fish in it, and gets on the noon bus back to Jerusalem. At four-thirty, when Eliahu and his brothers arrive, the frying pan is already sizzling in anticipation of them. They eat and talk about life and the world, and sometimes about their house in Zaku, where the river water would come up to the door in the winter. Now more and more Israeli Kurds go there because they miss it. It's a twilight area politically, partially autonomous. Ever since the Americans forbade the Iraqis to fly over the Kurdish area, the Kurds go in groups from Israel to the Turkish-Iraqi border. Near the town of Jezira they pay fifteen dollars and enter Iraq. A taxi takes them in and they visit their homes in Zaku, see and talk with the old neighbors, anoint themselves with that fragrance they will never forget. Efrayim's neighbor even photographed the entire Jewish neighborhood there with a video camera, and when he returned to Jerusalem he sold copies for 150 shekels apiece, and everyone saw the houses and the bridge, the river and the trees, and cried. Efrayim plans to go there sometime, make a twelve-day trip of it. He's already been in Egypt and Turkey and has danced with belly dancers, but he has not seen his birthplace, Zaku, since he left it.

When I ask when he plans to go, he tells me, "Patience, I'll go." He's in no hurry and doesn't think about death. When it comes, everything will be ready. He has a grave of his own beside his wife's grave; he bought them both at the same time. There's also a grave-stone with his name and year of birth; only the year of death is still to be engraved. "If you move the grave-stone just a foot or so, you see the pit. Father goes to care for Mother's grave and checks his own. Sometimes he climbs inside, to measure it, or to make sure there isn't another person there instead of him," Eli says and smiles.

After we guests leave Efrayim Zaken's house, toward evening, he goes to the synagogue, and at nine he goes to sleep for a few hours on the bed on the porch, in the wind, a bag with his electric bills and identity card under his head and the ax at his side. When he wakes up, around midnight, he prepares himself a glass of tea and goes out for a short walk. It's already happened that a friend of Eli's has been shocked to see him walking around the German Colony at two in the morning. To keep his strength up at night Efrayim has a slice of bread spread with butter and sugar. When the sun comes up and a few of the birds on the fig tree wake up, he checks the trees in the garden, waters, if necessary, the onions or the tobacco, then pours tehina into a plate, adds jelly, and eats. He begins a new day, as sweet as the last.

THE SON OF THE
FOREST GUARD

THE MAN WHO GUARDED the woods by the Heletz oil fields for twenty-five years had a son who set a fire in the forest, close to his father's cabin. "The motive for the deed is not clear," stated the brief police report. The matter was, so I discovered, a complicated one, with roots planted deep, thirty years before the event. At the center of the story is not the son, who was detained until his actions could be investigated, but rather the father, a large, stocky man. His language is picturesque and stimulating and he has a bad foot, such that he can no longer mount his horse and patrol the wood, which at night is full of voices and noises, motion and encounters. I drove south to meet the officer who investigated the acts of arson, in which, over the space of an entire month, small patches of forest close to the sheep farm were destroyed.

The police station in the desert town was small, a one-story building. At the entrance, on a bench, sat an Ethiopian woman whose neck was covered with a chain of blue tattooed crosses, and beside her sat two Russian youths. The desk sergeant snoozed under a picture of the president. Next to him was the iron door of the local detention cell, punctured by a tiny peephole. A fire extinguisher and related equipment stood in one corner. The walls were painted with high-gloss paint up to eye level. A large party was about to commence in one of the town's wedding halls, and the policemen had been invited. The captain was running around town and couldn't be found. I left town and continued on to the guard's place via the road that goes through the Ivim woods. The November sun warmed a field of cabbage and a eucalyptus grove, a wheat field and a puddle left over from the last rain. The hills were soft to the eye and the air was sweet and crisp. Right at the road sign for Lapidot a short dirt road veered off sharply to the right, and I entered a small camp surrounded by a fence. Two dogs rose from their sprawl and bared their teeth. I saw a young mare and a goose, hens and donkeys. A large, mustachioed man emerged from an asbestos cabin, his broad face one that could look pleasant to a guest or frightening to an invader. "As peaceful as it may seem," he told me right off, as if making a preliminary report on the situation, "there's a war going on here."

We sat under an awning, in view of a clock with one hand and a white telephone, a few chairs and a table set with an electric kettle and coffee cups. Everything looked like a laid-back rural retreat that in its better days might have hosted its neighbor, General (ret.) Ariel Sharon of the adjacent Ha-Shikmim Farm, as well as policemen and Bedouin. Now the place was very quiet and only the excitement of a stranger's visit caused some of the roosters to crow for a while. After the noise died down, the guard, David, spoke. At first only a bit, and with brevity, and afterwards in the great outpouring of one who has had things sitting inside him and who is accustomed to long conversations under a roof made of wooden beams and netting. His son, Amir, was not there. He had been arrested and taken to Eitanim Hospital for observation. The animals, all of them his, waited for him with the patience of beasts who have sufficient food and water.

"It wasn't my son who set the fire," the guard said plainly. "For two of the fires he was even in a different city. Why would he set a fire next to his sheep pen, next to his father and mother? If the fire took hold, it would have consumed them and everything else. It's like me going and setting fire to my own bread box and bed." The guard wore a Royal Indian Club T-shirt; his lame leg was extended in front of him and he held a denuded walking stick in his hand. An aged man, quite skinny, with blue eyes, also sat with us. He was responsible for the orchards. He had come "just to see if David was still alive." The skinny man had spent decades walking "these thousand acres, which were once almonds but are now pasture and forage." He has a small shack, close to that of the guard, but he doesn't sleep there, as David does; he sleeps in his house in Nes Tziona.

The Heletz region is a broad swathe of land on the

edge of the desert, far from the center of the country, and wild. David waved his hand in a large circle. "Here," he said, "my son Amir and the boy across the road divided the land, part for one and part for the other, just like you and I might decide to share out the sea." Three farms lie in view of each other in Heletz, set up on land that, at the time, looked as if it were unclaimed. The guard's son settled on a territory at the foot of the phone company's antenna hill. He had six hundred sheep there and a shack for himself and the Bedouin who were with him. On an adjacent hill, next to an oil drill, was another fellow, a young man who had had some problems with the law, in Israel and abroad. He gave up the city, took a hill, and put a trailer on it, and then a few other structures and a sheep pen. He has a beautiful daughter he's anxious about; she goes to school off the farm. He has a wife who came from Europe and five more small children who live among the sheep. His farm looks like a rough Gypsy camp. Fences and junk, the remains of a flag, and disturbing piles of sheep bones in two pits, testimony to a slaughter. A third farm lies further down the dirt road that descends from the sheep-bone pits. Beyond that, on another hill, is the oil-prospecting camp. There are a few rigs there and a huge drill.

The guard's son and the second farmer divided the pasture land between them, one north, one south. There was the usual sheepherder's dispute between them. "There were people who wanted our pasture land, who wanted our sheep out of here. Maybe that's where the

fire came from." Years ago David discovered a huge
field of marijuana plants on some land between two kib-
butzim. There was a bed with easily two thousand
plants in the Shikma River channel. "Maybe those guys
got mad at me. There are Arabs I kept from killing
Francis, who I found bleeding in his car after they hit
him over the head with a hoe. Maybe that's where the
fire came from. There are thieves here and drug dealers,
and there are Gazans and Bedouin." The forest ranger
spent a long time talking about the area, and the seem-
ingly simple territory quickly came to sound like some
sort of no-man's-land that everyone was grabbing for,
with threats of vengeance hovering over it like a poison
miasma. "A lot of people had an interest in seeing me
get fucked over." Maybe because he has lived here for
many years already and his eyes are open. More than
once he's reported criminal activity, even if anony-
mously, and he had as many enemies as he had friends.
Why would his son go out and set fire to the four
corners of the woods that surrounded his father's little
estate, not to mention the sheep pen that he himself
lived in?

After our first meeting, I in fact asked myself why a
son would get up and set fire to the woods next to his
father's house. What lies hidden in the love of a father
and a son that can kindle a conflagration? "Even in his
cell," the police officer told me when I located him and
he rushed over to the guard's shelter in his little Peugot.
"Amir set a fire even in his cell at the station. He burned
a newspaper, and the duty officer smelled smoke and we

---

went in and put out the fire. He also shouted 'God is great' in Arabic." The officer's inclination was to pass over that in silence, because he already knew what I did not yet know—that Amir was the guard's son by the Bedouin woman Latifa, and that this whole matter of the fire had been smoldering for many years, since the guard himself had been a boy in Yavna'el.

Under the awning, the yellow dog resting at his feet, as the guard began telling me about his life, he wondered what connection it had with his son. He had been born in Alexandria, Egypt, on the beach. His family, which came there from Europe, had lived there for four generations. His parents spoke Italian, French, and Greek, everything but Arabic. When he was nine years old, they moved to Israel, itself a year-old infant, and settled in Yavna'el. Playing outside on the slope of the mountain, near the Bedouin tents, David met Bedouin kids and made friends with the children of a family whose mother had died of malaria. They were his age, and among them was an eleven-year-old girl named Latifa. They became like brother and sister, young soulmates, and he learned Arabic from her.

When, some years later, he met the girl from Yavna'el who would be his first wife, the Bedouin girl Latifa was their chaperone when they went out together. He was still very young when he married. He worked as a metalworker and a tractor driver and threw his strong back into all sorts of other work. They had three children—his eldest son and two girls. When he couldn't find work in the mid-1960s and was in tough financial straits, he heard that they were looking for a field guard for the Kadoorie agricultural school and went there. He'd always wanted to be alone, just himself and the animals and the fields. When he began the guarding job, he found that he had indeed found happiness. For there, close by, on the slopes of Mount Tabor, he again met—"because it was fated"—the Bedouin family he had known as a boy. They had wandered with their sheep and were at that time in Arab el-Shibli, at the foot of Mount Tabor. The girl he had loved as a sister was with them, and it was there that their romance began.

From his place in the field, he established a private sign language with her and began to signal her with a broken mirror. He signaled when he wanted to meet with her and she would go out as if to wash the silver coffee tray. She'd move it in such a way as to send a flash of reply. They met at night while he was on guard duty and made out in his guard's shack. It wasn't long before her belly began to swell. Hidden in her loose dresses, she took care not to be caught, because she knew that would bring great disaster on her. But when her fingers got crushed by a stone and she was taken to the doctor, her pregnancy was discovered. She was taken back home, and David understood from people he knew in the village that her life was in danger. An old man was brought to the house to marry her immediately. Latifa was sent to the kitchen to prepare coffee. In order to signify that she agreed to marry the man, she had to take the elderly guest's coffee to him and offer it from her hands to his. This she would not do, because she didn't want him, and then and there her brothers decided to do away with her.

They consulted and agreed that on Saturday morning Latifa would go up to the roof while they prepared a barrel of tar on a fire below. The tar would be brought up in buckets to where she worked, on the roof, and her little brother would be the one to push her off the side facing the slope of the high, rocky mountain. That was how she would die. But the little brother didn't do as he was ordered, and when Latifa finished tarring the roof, she went down. Meanwhile, sitting in the Kadoorie fields, David was watching the Bedouin village—and his girlfriend's house—with binoculars. He saw her tarring the roof and descending, healthy and whole. He was twenty-six years old and his stomach was turning over with worry. When she climbed down, she disappeared from his view. That was when she entered the little kitchen, which was a small shack in the yard of the Bedouin house. Her oldest brother was inside. "Why didn't you serve coffee to the guest who was here last night?" he asked her. She answered what she answered and he dealt her a blow on the head with the ax he had in his hand. Her hand was broken when she tried to shield her face, and she fell, bleeding, on the floor and lost consciousness. When she woke up, she found she was in a dark, close place, unable to move. Her brothers had wrapped her in a blood-soaked tarpaulin, thrown her into a septic pit they'd dug in the yard, and covered her with stones and dirt. She'd been buried for many hours by the time David called the police, who came and dug and found the poor girl alive, if barely breathing, and the baby in her womb alive as well.

She recovered slowly in the hospital in Afula. When she rose from her bed, David took her to keep her far away from her brothers. The brother who had struck her was tried and sentenced to several years in prison. The couple moved to a different city, where David found guard work, far from the tribe that pursued his lover. They lived in a shack between the empty houses of an abandoned village, and when her labor began, they went to the hospital and their first child was born—the one who had been saved by a miracle from his mother's grave in the Bedouin village. They were very poor, because his entire guard's salary went to his wife and his children in Yavna'el, and they were forced to give the beautiful baby, dark like her mother, up for adoption.

For years David and Latifa lived in orchards and vineyards, in guard shacks here and there, in Beit Shemesh and Neve Tamar, in pup tents and broken-down huts, in cold and poverty. Their second daughter was born in the Heletz camp. David rode happily on his horse, circuiting each day on his patrol the thousand acres of orchards. Starting in the months from when the trees first bloomed until the fruit was picked, he guarded with care, equipped with a hunting rifle and a pistol, and more than once captured thieves and infiltrators. Once he even caught an Egyptian spy who was hiding in the orchards with a Gaza seaman. They were either escaping someone or had come to peek at the oil drilling. When there was no fruit to guard, he would migrate for a few months to a different city, and even went as far as Sinai. His son Amir was born in Heletz and was circumcised as a Jewish boy. The mother moved with the two children to live in a small town in the north, because David again wanted to live alone—that was the life he knew. When Amir was just six years old, he was already making the trip on his own by bus from the north. When the bus passed by the guard's shack, close to the road, the pointer bitch would bark and David would know that his son had arrived. Like his father, the boy hated the city from the start and saw it as a curse. His mother would take him the three miles by bus to kindergarten, and when she got home she'd find him sitting on the steps waiting for her. He had fled on foot as soon as she left.

The boy always liked animals more than people. "Here," David told me, "the three geese are my son's. None of them produces and one of them is old and lame. There are also old hens here, because we don't put the animals we raise into the pot. My son Amir loves animals so much that he won't even kill a ewe that's broken her leg. He says: A person who's broken his leg goes to the doctor and they don't shoot him. He ties up the broken leg with a plastic drip-irrigation pipe until the fracture heals, especially if it's a front foot. But old sheep," the elderly guard said, perhaps thinking of himself, "their feet don't heal until they die." There was a black mare and a colt and a white donkey and a little brown donkey and five dogs, all of them somehow living together without making a racket—except for the rooster, who clearly felt himself the master of the house.

From childhood, Amir loved the Heletz region, and would walk at his father's side, searching for footprints. A boy of fields and orchards and creatures. At the age of fourteen he was thrown out of his school in the north and came finally to live with his father. He wanted orchards and a tractor and a horse of his own. But one day, while he was driving someone's tractor, the vehicle over-turned and crushed the boy. "At the hospital they told me he was dead, and I thought the whole time about where we would bury him, with the Jews or the Arabs? Both would ostracize him. His mother's family had cut off all contact and kept them under a ban, but how could a boy who was legally Bedouin be buried in a Jewish cemetery?" But the boy, like his mother, came back from the dead, and when he was recovered he worked like a madman, operating agricultural vehicles for one of the local growers, tractor and disc and plow, and in the afternoon he would ride alongside his father on a horse. Every time they tried to close him in he ran away, first from kindergarten, and afterwards from school, and then from the city altogether; and when he was in the hospital after the tractor accident, he tried to run away from there, too. Even when he was hospitalized with Malta fever, a horrible disease caught from sheep, once more he tried to run away. He also ran away from the open psychiatric ward at the Eitanim hospital after his arrest.

For years Amir lived alongside his father in Heletz. There are two beds beside each other in the little shack, where everything is neat and clean to guard against mice. But when he grew up he rebelled against his father and they had the kinds of arguments that fathers and sons have, and there were also all the tribulations of a boy whose mother comes from the Bedouin and whose father is a Jew. One week he was an Arab and one week he was a Jew, now on this side and now on that side. And all the time people came to the shack, his father's friends, and they spoke half the night, and Arab and Bedouin workers would come by also, always in a different mood, as David says, according to what had happened that day—if a Jew was killed by an Arab or an Arab by a Jew, if there was a massacre here or there. A split personality was imposed on the guard's son, who spoke Arabic and Hebrew as his mother and father tongues and who was attracted to both sides of the divide. He was connected to both by blood, and in his heart. And that was enough to conflict a person's mind. Then, two weeks before the fire, policemen and inspectors came and took all six hundred of the sheep he so loved, because some of them had shown signs of Malta fever and the herd had to be destroyed. It's a disease that some sheep raisers try to hide so that their entire flocks will not be destroyed. There are those who, even when they themselves come down with the fever, which causes waves of hot and cold, go to be treated in an Arab hospital in Hebron so that their condition will not be reported in Israel and their sheep taken from them.

David pleaded with me to come with him to the place the fire started, so that I could see with my own eyes how small and harmless it had been and how could it possibly be that his son would set it so close to his own sheep. Giant radio antennas stood on the hill, and the ranger's guard tower stood on another hill. Piles of hay were hidden under tarpaulins, and a large pen stood empty. Nearby was the shack of his son Amir, where he lived with his mother, who had moved here for a while, and the Bedouin shepherd family Abu Shuloof. Everything was black and sooty from the campfire. "When my son wasn't with the sheep, he always sat in front of a ring of fire, watching it as if it were his television. Here's where we prepared food." Facing the fire, the source of simple existence, Amir returned to Bedouin life as if he had never lived anywhere else. The smell of smoke and sheep and hay, and that's all. Perhaps that is the fire that captured his heart as a solution to the knot of his life.

Five months after the son's arrest I found a short message on my e-mail from the man who had first told me about the guard's son. "I regret to inform you that the son of the forest guard whom you visited at Heletz today put an end to his life by hanging himself in his cell."

I EZ

EZRA ANGEL, who sits and tells me about his happy kibbutz days of forty years ago—he's listing, in detail, all
the necessary ingredients in the preparation of cattle
feed—looks like a man who has returned from the dead.
I first met him half a year earlier, when he was still
among the dead, or, more correctly, among the missing,
languishing in the yard of a madhouse. That's where I
heard a story that could make even those who have
heard everything shiver.

He was born to a Jewish family in the Syrian city
of Haleb, and when he had grown some, he was sent
secretly, by way of a smuggler, into the young country
of Israel. There he was to settle, alone, and wait for his
parents. After being smuggled in, he lived for a few
years as part of a youth contingent under the care of a

kibbutz that had adopted him. He grew into a muscular youth, strong as the Biblical Samson, who dreamed always of returning to Syria to deliver his mother, who had not come after him.

When he reached military age, he went, with his kibbutz buddies, into the army. One summer, while he was in an NCO course, he paid a visit to friends who were living in a kibbutz on the Syrian border. Angel told them that he had decided to go free his mother from Haleb. The friends, who had a feeling that he wasn't joking, tried to deter him from his insane plan. Everyone knew of the Syrians' cruelty and the way they treated Israelis who fell into their hands. One morning Ezra, dressed in his gym clothes, disappeared, not to be seen again for many years. Crossing the border with the naïveté of a boy whose longing for his mother overwhelmed his fears, he was captured by the Syrians. For nine years he was beaten and humiliated in a scorching cell in the desert prison of Tadmor. He was held there with other Israelis who had crossed for a variety of reasons, or had unintentionally wandered over, or had been kidnaped, and no one in Israel knew what had happened to them. When he was returned, along with seven other prisoners, all of them shells of human beings, he was taken to a psychiatric hospital for examination. Thirty-one years later he was still confined. The week he was returned from his Syrian imprisonment they fixed the madman label on him, and he bore it like a cross of agony all his life. Forgotten by all, he was hauled from here to there and back again, transferred from one hospital to another, up to his ears in psychoactive drugs powerful enough to drive a sane man out of his mind, all the while accompanied by a thin medical file that was little more than a catalogue of misdiagnoses that amounted to a stigma imposing a punishment on him equal to three life sentences.

The fate of most of the people who had been in the Syrian prison with him was no better than his. Some of them, as I discovered after I found him, died in the hospitals and were buried who knows where, and others, with few exceptions, remained hospitalized as he was. I approached this story with a certain trepidation, yet from the time I heard and saw Angel, I felt positively ensnared, because here is stark evidence of a dark chamber that exists even in a democratic country where everything is ostensibly well-lit and open. Yes, there *are* people who got ejected from life into the psychiatric hospitalization system and who disappeared inside bearing erroneous labels, erased from life, and their cries were not—were never—heard.

For Angel the miracle came late. His brother's daughter arrived from Europe, where she had lived for years, having decided to find her vanished uncle. When she located him she was, initially, terrified by his toothless appearance. On the spot she declared a miniature war against everyone and worked to deliver Uncle Ezra. She discovered that her uncle did not appear in the government's computer under his correct name, that he had no identity card, that his army dossier was missing, that he had been dropped from the national census rolls, that money that he should have received as his part in his inheritance from his mother had been appropriated by the state's administrator general, and that a blind trust that was supposed to provide for all his needs yet had done very little. She searched for a trustee by the name of Tzuriel but could find no one with that name. It took her months to get an identity card for her uncle, to extract him from the institution he'd been in, and to construct an official identity for him. I became aware of the story only at the end of his great ordeals, and I went with the niece to the hospital to see her uncle.

We passed under bridges that bore blood-red banners boasting "Our Soldiers Will Never Be Abandoned," alongside graffiti proclaiming "Nightmarish Peace" and "Leave Gaza Now." It had taken Dana two months to extract Ezra from the institution he'd been in when she found him. A private institution for chronic patients, surrounded by greenery, in which Angel lived as a vegetable waiting for feeding times. She heard of a psychiatrist named Bastiaans in Beersheba and immediately wanted her uncle to be transferred to his clinic. Bastiaans' father had gained fame for his method of treating Holocaust survivors, using psychoactive drugs that returned them to the death camps, so that they could be taken out of them once and for all. Bastiaans the younger carried on his father's work concentrating on the treatment of traumas that imprison their victims for the rest of their lives behind what he calls "a private barbed-wire fence."

When Bastiaans read about the prisoner Angel, he thought that the long and cruel imprisonment and the endless period of hospitalization were similar to the cases of Holocaust survivors. He thought that to save him might be like saving a Holocaust survivor. Angel was taken out of the private institution, his few belongings were packed, and he was transferred in an ambulance to Bastiaans' clinic. He crossed the country on his way to the unknown, already accustomed to being hauled off every few years without anyone telling him where to or why. Before he departed, someone at the private hospital told him that he'd have no food in the south, that he'd go hungry. He was frightened and very worried. At the edge of Beersheba he was taken into the Ben-Gurion University psychiatric hospital and given a room. Bastiaans quickly came to see him. The doctor was tall and good-looking, with a light goatee that had gone gray from endless battles with every bureaucrat who crossed his path. The battle heat he'd brought with him to Israel from Holland had been exchanged over the years for headaches and neck pains. When Bastiaans examined Angel's medical file, he was flabbergasted: according to the photocopied documents he'd received, Angel had been diagnosed as schizophrenic just two days after his return to Israel together with the other prisoners. It said in the file that the prisoner Angel was catatonic. He had arrived bent over in acute fear, and just like anyone who receives deadly blows, who has been conditioned that way, like a Holocaust survivor, he had displayed no emotion. He was in that robotic state the Nazis called the "discipline of a corpse."

"These are people who discovered, as they tried to survive, that any expression of emotion could mean death," Bastiaans told me as I sat in his office while he stood, restlessly, angry, swinging between wrath and astonishment. "The prisoners knew that they were forbidden to look in the eyes of their jailers. I wasn't there when he returned from Syria, but I've seen a photograph of him on his return and it speaks volumes. My assistant, Dr. Zugman, was with me. He spent years in Siberia and cared for Russian prisoners of war who came back. He said to me, 'I know this man,' and he meant the person who returns from the inferno. You see the horrible tension, the cringing. The person is frozen and hunched over to defend himself. I have the summary report on his illness from the hospital in Acre. An anthology of psychiatric blunders. I'll tell you the problem with our profession: we plagiarize. Angel lived with that initial diagnosis for thirty years, and when he arrived here, what I saw facing me was what we call 'the final artificial result of erroneous psychiatric care.'" The psychiatrist held himself back from excoriating his colleagues any further. He is a man of culture, burning with his own agonies and those of others.

After Uncle Ezra was transferred to Bastiaans, his brother's daughter came to see him. He was very thin, still frightened, and his blood pressure had shot up. After years as an anonymous patient, Angel had all of a sudden been transferred to such a different ward. The staff began examining him as if he had just this moment gotten out of the Syrian prison, as if no thirty years during which he had borne on his back the diagnosis of schizophrenia had intervened. Bastiaans wanted to act quickly to change the patient's condition, and the niece was pressing him, eager for some sort of immediate redemption. But the Russian psychiatrist, Zugman, insisted that it was vital that they proceed very slowly. "We're dealing here," said Zugman, "with a man who has been in prison for forty years. It won't be simple to prove whether the previous clinicians erred or not. Things are erased, they change. Time obscures so much. Beatings and medications, endless hospitalization, high blood pressure and diabetes, loss of teeth and bad food—these things have devastated him. We need some new proof of the origin of the disease, to connect it to the imprisonment in Syria, in order to change the treatment, get rid of the labels, improve Angel's future quality of life."

The work done by Bastiaans and his deputies was like the work of detectives assigned by a commission of inquiry to solve an old crime. Go try to separate the blows the Syrians gave him from the damage caused by thirty years of medical imprisonment. They set out to find the specific cause of Angel's deterioration and where the key to his recovery lay. They sought a broken bone, a fracture, dead cells, a blockage, an accumulation of harmful substances.

Of course there also remained the troublesome question of why an eighteen-year-old boy would seek to cross the border to free his mother. Did he already, at that time, have trouble making judgments about reality? Was he ill, or simply a youth wracked by longing? Bastiaans and his deputy questioned at length a friend of Angel's who came to the hospital to visit him—Kini, who had known him in the years before his border crossing, when they were both parentless young kids at Kibbutz Alonin. Kini remembered Angel as a very strong boy who could pick up railroad tracks—not disturbed, just missing his mother a great deal. "When he crossed the border, none of us saw him as a traitor or lunatic. We were orphans ourselves, and we knew what it was like to miss a mother." A second possible explanation of Ezra's current state was the effect of his extended hospitalization. Any person, even a healthy one, will become sick if he is hospitalized for too long, even if he was not sick to begin with. A third possibility, and the one that seemed the most likely to Bastiaans, was that there was brain damage.

Bastiaans explained to me that he had yet to examine a Holocaust survivor who had come out of the camps without brain damage, from beatings and bashings and undernourishment. To check for this possibility after a delay of so many years, he planned out a series of skull and neck X-rays and a CAT scan. During a session in Bastiaans' office, Angel drew some particularly disturbing pictures. In drawings of people he emphasized the eyes, but they were nothing more than empty sockets. He drew a house and a tree. The house didn't look like a house and the tree had no ground under it. "A tree without ground is a detached person." There's a pretty concise description of Angel.

The bleak vastness of the desert stretched beyond the hospital fence, and the garden extended out only as far as the irrigation pipe ran. A boy came and sat next to me in the garden as I waited for Uncle Ezra; he asked me for the rest of the ice cream cone I was licking. It was tranquil in ward 20, where Bastiaans worked with a team that nicely complemented his personality. There was his Russian deputy, Zugman, who came from the Siberan camps, and the resident Henri, who had come to Israel from France. He played the guitar for the patients, sang in operas, and lived with a wife and three small children in an absolutely empty apartment. Henri was the one who took Uncle Ezra for his head examination. In ward 20, Angel received, for the first time in his life, a private room, with a cabinet and a chair, all to himself. During his long years in institutions—prison and hospitals—he had lived in rooms with eight or ten other people, sharing a feces-smeared toilet with them, the same sink, even the same sponge and soap, and the same razor, tied to the faucet.

Angel had touched Henri's heart. Henri wanted to get closer to him and would sit by him and the occupational therapist, Mathilda, with whom Angel sometimes danced when they put music on. Henri sat and Angel was silent. Henri asked Angel, "Do you like me?" "No, I don't like you." "Do you hate me?" "No, I don't hate you." That's how they spoke the first time. Henri discovered that Angel took an interest in food and the army, in father and mother, and that all this was connected for him. Ezra told him that he had crossed over to Syria to bring food to his mother. After so many years in institutions, food had become his sole interest.

Food and cigarettes, which everyone smoked to pass the time that had no end. When they sat together, waiting in the line for the skull examination, Henri said to Angel: "You smoke so much that it'll damage your health." "I don't have lungs," Angel said. "You've got lungs, just like all human beings do," Henri said. "I am not a human being. I ez," Angel said and fell silent. The brother's daughter was afraid that here he'd slipped back into madness, but after a few days Angel told her that his mother used to call him Ez instead of Ezra.

A few weeks went by before Angel opened up. He was like a baby learning new things, except that with a baby all the doors are wide open while with Angel all of them had been slammed shut for years and years. The staff went right at him with new stimuli, they touched him and played music, sang and spoke—but they found that he was only withdrawing further. Patients like Angel and Holocaust survivors always have a barbed-wire fence they put up around themselves for defense. Their souls require it. It takes time to build the right network of stimuli to make a positive connection. Ezra's sugar count shot up and his blood pressure went crazy. The body reacted. They weaned him from his medication and that worked like drug detoxification. It took six months for his body to get used to it. It's a dangerous process. If you do it too quickly, there's a boomerang affect. Angel had violent thoughts and they understood that they were going too fast. They concluded that he would continue to need some sort of antipsychotic medication, probably indefinitely. The nurses touched him, came close to him, combed his hair. He was bombarded with warmth and affection and still he retreated inward. In time, he opened up and responded for brief periods. Once, he excitedly watched the Independence Day ceremony. Another morning he suddenly began to sing, and they discovered that he had a pleasant voice. But when he was sent to the physiotherapists, he closed up because they touched his body. From within his ossification sleeping emotions began to waken. They learned that he had to be treated with great care and allowed to let things out slowly. When you come back to life you are animal-like, like a monster baby—you have to be taught everything from scratch.

His old friend Kini came to visit him. At first they were quiet and then they began to talk. Kini, who was Ezra's good friend at the kibbutz, and then also at Hulata, the place he'd disappeared from, had become a union leader. He tried to draw him out, tried to heal him with human contact. He took him to the movies, but Ezra got upset by something all of a sudden and insisted on going home, and Kini realized how much patience would be required of anyone who hoped to connect Ezra to the world. The brother's daughter came from France every month. Once she took Ezra with her to a hotel on the Dead Sea, hoping that her uncle might be reborn out of the therapeutic warm mud. He went down with her to the warm pool and gave himself over to the pleasure. In the lobby he looked at people and talked about the food as if he were fearful that all that abundance could suddenly disappear.

The last time I visited Angel and his niece, Ezra took us to a place he called the "canteen." His vocabulary had frozen forty years ago. The formula he began to give us for cattle fodder was also from 1953. His shampooed hair stood up like nails on his scalp while he gave the girl who worked in the canteen instructions on how to prepare the simple food that he liked. He jealously guarded a box of Lipton tea he'd bought so that he could make himself better tea than the ward offered. "I don't dream about anything," he told me. "I would like to plow and raise wheat like I did at the kibbutz. Anyone who likes bread like I do works good with wheat." As he spoke, the names of the friends he'd worked with in the field came back to him, along with the smell of the chickens they used to steal and cook in their room. He recalled the wonderful feeling of plowing in a dry field.

A month after that visit his friend Kini called me all upset and told me that Ezra had disappeared from the hospital. It took me some time to discover that the brother's daughter had spirited him out of the country. Just as he had suddenly turned up one day in Syria, he'd suddenly turned up in France—in Nice. The brother's daughter dreamed that in a new place he'd return to himself and would be a new man. Left behind at the hospital was his thick medical file, the entire wretched chronicle, as well as a slender little school notebook in which he had recorded, in a childish hand, all his petty daily expenses, and also everything that had happened to him since he'd been found.

ABOUT THE AUTHOR

Igal Sarna was born in 1952 and served as a tank commander in the Yom Kippur War in 1973. He writes for the daily newspaper *Yediot Aharonot* and was one of the founders of the Peace Now movement. He received the IBM Tolerance Prize for a series of cover stories on Iranian political prisoners in Israel, and in 1998 he was awarded a Fulbright grant and spent a semester at the University of Iowa International Writing Program. He has published, in Hebrew, a biography of the poet Yona Wallach and a novel, *Tzayad Ha-Zikaron (Hunter of Memory)*. He lives in Tel Aviv with his wife and two children.

ABOUT THE TRANSLATOR

Haim Watzman is a translator and journalist who lives in Jerusalem with his wife and four children. His translations include David Grossman's *The Yellow Wind* and *Sleeping on a Wire* and Tom Segev's *The Seventh Million* and *One Palestine, Complete.*